RICHARD AKEHURST

SPORTING GUNS

OCTOPUS BOOKS

Acknowledgements

The publishers would like to thank the following people for giving access to their collections:
Figures 2, 3, 4, 5, 6, 7, 8, 10, 11, 12, 13, 14, 15, 16, 17, 18, 20, 21, 22, 23, 24, 26, 27, 28, 30, 31, 33, 34, 35, 36, 37, 38, 39, 40, 41, 43, 44, 45, 46, 47, 48, 49, 51, 52, 53, 54, 59, W. Keith Neal Esq.; figures 42, 57, 62, 63, 64, 66, 71, 76, 77, 78, 81, 85, 88, 89, 105, 106, 107, 108, 114, 115, 123, 129, 132, Richard Akehurst Esq.; figures 79, 109, 120, 121, 122, Frank Anderson Esq.; figures 116, 117, 119, Atkin Grant and Lang Ltd.; figures 72, 87, John Bates Esq.; figures 83, 97, The Marquess of Bath; figures 130, 131, Gordon Colquhoun Esq.; figures 95, 111, James Purdey & Sons Ltd.
The publishers and author would also like to thank the following people for taking the photographs:
Figures 1, 2, 3, 4, 5, 6, 7, 8, 9, 10, 11, 12, 13, 14, 15, 16, 17, 18, 19, 20, 21, 22, 23, 24, 26, 27, 28, 29, 30, 31, 32, 33, 34, 35, 36, 37, 38, 39, 40, 41, 43, 45, 46, 47, 48, 49, 50, 51, 52, 53, 54, 59, W. Keith Neal Esq.; figures 130, 131, C. O'Brien Esq.; figures 83, 97, Douglas Byles Esq.; figures 6, 44, 55, 56, 58, 60, 61, 62, 63, 64, 65, 66, 67, 68, 69, 70, 72, 73, 74, 75, 77, 79, 80, 81, 82, 84, 85, 86, 87, 88, 89, 90, 91, 92, 93, 94, 96, 98, 99, 100, 101, 102, 103, 104, 105, 106, 107, 109, 110, 111, 112, 113, 115, 116, 117, 118, 119, 120, 121, 122, 124, 125, 126, 127, 128, 132, 133, C. Crosthwaite Esq.

Preceding page
Duck shooting, coloured aquatint *c.* 1850

Contents page
Gunmaker's trade plate,
wood engraving by Thomas Bewick

This edition first published 1972 by
OCTOPUS BOOKS LIMITED
59 Grosvenor Street, London W.1

ISBN 7064 0031 3

PRODUCED BY MANDARIN PUBLISHERS LIMITED AND PRINTED IN HONG KONG

Contents

1 Duck shooting in winter showing peasantry with match-lock guns, powder flasks and priming flasks. Sepia drawing by Stradanus, c. 1566

Sixteenth Century

2 Match-lock gun showing reverse side of butt with engraved bone inlay

BY the sixteenth century the hand gun had been developed to a form where it could be aimed and handled reasonably well. Both the peasantry and aristocracy of Europe were quick to appreciate its advantages over the bow for certain types of hunting: the peasantry could now shoot a wider variety of fowl, since their guns were loaded with small shot which gave a fair spread. As for the aristocracy the matchlock gun [figure 3] and later the matchlock rifle proved more powerful than the crossbow and replaced it for use against the larger animals which still abounded in the forests of Europe.

The use of guns for shooting fowl in England is first mentioned in statutes passed in the reign of Henry VIII. Up to his reign, archers had been the backbone of the army and earlier acts had tried to maintain the importance of the long bow by forbidding the use of guns without a special licence granted by the king. However by 1537 the advantages of the guns were recognized and a limited force was trained in their use; the Guild of Saint George, now known as the Honourable Artillery Company of London, was formed about that time. The statute authorizing its formation contains a provision of particular interest which permitted the use of hand guns for shooting at marks and butts, and at all game and fowl.

The gun referred to was the matchlock arquebus. Permission for such non-military use was no doubt a privilege granted in return for service; but since it encouraged marksmanship and the development of guile and strategy in approaching a wary quarry, it had a natural application to the arts of war.

In 1542 citizens and landowners too were permitted the use of guns, but only to practise marksmanship: at the same time the widespread and illegal use of firearms was deplored. (It is interesting to note that the keepers of forests, parks and chases had, by this time, put aside the long bow in favour of the gun.) The Act of 1542 further laid down that no bird or animal might be hunted by anyone without a royal licence. This licence could be obtained only by a per-

5

3 Match-lock gun, probably Dutch c. 1590,
showing detail of lock but without the slow-
match cord

son with an income of one hundred pounds or over, who then had to deposit with the King's courts of Chancery the sum of twenty pounds; this bond was forfeited if the person was convicted of contravening the laws of game, guns and trespass; or alternatively, if he shot game not specifically covered by the licence.

In spite of these official measures to restrict fowling, the illegal use of guns was widespread. For years country men had been supplementing their stocks of food in winter with any fowl that came within range of their guns [figure 1].

The barrels for these matchlock guns were probably made by local blacksmiths from iron folded and welded longitudinally round a mandril. The simplest lock used was of the serpentine type, while the better guns had locks of the sear type. The local carpenter possibly made the gun stocks, but some were probably home made.

The powder was of two types; coarse for the main charge and fine for priming. The shot (known then as 'hail' shot) was made by clipping small squares of lead from a sheet, which were then rounded by tumbling over and over in a barrel or jar. For wadding tow, rag or paper was used. In the matchlock guns, the powder was ignited by a constantly burning 'match' held in the lock. When the gun was in use the smouldering slow match had to be moved forward constantly in the serpentine as it burned back, so that it would be in the right position when the gun was fired to fall onto the priming powder in the pan, thereby igniting the main charge through the touch hole.

Fowlers relied on stalking sitting birds because shooting at flying birds was out of the question. They sometimes used a specially trained stalking horse which acted as a screen,

5 Small bore German wheel-lock gun *c.* 1590, showing wheel with square axis end to take the key, and the jaw that holds the iron pyrites

while at other times they used a cloth and wood screen to simulate a horse. Another wily technique to fill the larder was to entice birds within range with corn. Such were the inauspicious beginnings of the sport of shooting in England.

On the continent of Europe, the invention, early in the sixteenth century, of the wheel-lock and of rifling in barrels gave impetus to the already established sport of shooting game. The advantages of these inventions were twofold: now that the smouldering match was dispensed with, stalking became much easier, since the gun could be carried safely and yet be ready for instant use; at the same time, the use of rifling considerably extended the range of accuracy.

Although Leonardo da Vinci did make drawings of a form of wheel-lock, its actual inventor remains unknown. As with most inventions, once the idea had been established, a number of different people developed it to the point of general application. Most of the early wheel-locks came from Nuremberg, for they are intricate mechanisms, and at first only the clock-makers of south Germany and northern Italy were skilled enough to make them. The wheel-lock [figure 5] works through the spinning of a serrated-edged wheel, which strikes sparks into the centre of the priming pan from a piece of iron pyrites held in place by

4 (*opposite*) Powder horn, French *c.* 1590. Henri IV on one side and his Queen and family on the other

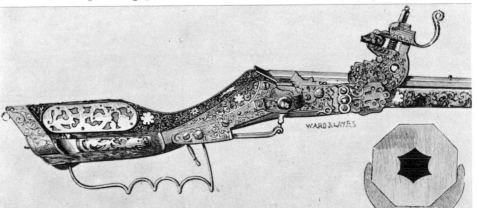

6 Wheel-lock tschinke, Bohemian *c.* 1650. Note the external mainspring

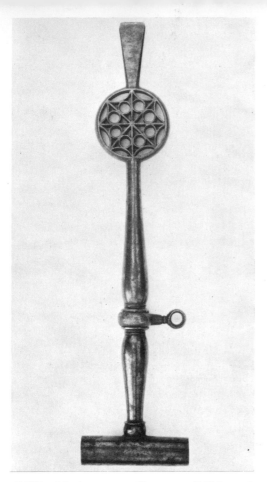

7 Wheel-lock spanner, German *c*. 1600, used for winding the lock spring

the jaws of the dog head. The wheel, connected to the V-shaped mainspring by a short chain, is brought under tension by means of a spanner or key [figure 7] which fits the square-shaped extension on the external axis of the wheel. For the gun to be carried safely the dog head must be swung back and held by its spring, and the priming pan covered.

King Henry VIII collected many fine examples of German, Italian and French wheel-locks including early breech-loading types. Fine wheel-lock rifles were used by the King and his courtiers for shooting at marks, or for the sport of popinjay which involved shooting at a model bird set up on a high pole. Some richly decorated pieces were preserved more for their decorative than their practical value. The English, however, still hunted the stag and hare with horse and hound.

On the continent an interesting small bore wheel-lock rifle with an external mainspring was developed in south-west Poland at the town now called Cieszyn, but then known as Teschen, from which this rifle derives it name, *tschinke* [figure 6]. These tschinkes were widely used for shooting game birds such as pheasants after they had been flushed into trees by dogs. As these rifles fired only a small ball with a light charge, the short butt could be held against the cheek in comfort, since the weight of the rifle was sufficient to take most of the recoil [figure 21].

In England however, fowling with a gun had not yet established itself as a sport or as a respectable form of hunting. Birds for the table of the gentry were taken by netting with the aid of dogs, while hawks and falcons were used for sport. Fowling with a gun was still too closely associated with the peasantry creeping up on their quarry and taking a 'pot shot'.

8 German wheel-lock gun, figure 5, showing reverse side of butt

Seventeenth Century

To the Honourable Thomas
R.t Hon.ble (Henry Lord Fairfax)
This Plate is humbly Dedicated

Fairfax Esq.r eldest Son of y.e
of Denton in York-shire
by Richard Blome.

9 An engraving from *The Gentleman's Recreation* 1686. The practice of shooting from horseback whilst servants reloaded the guns, was largely confined to the seventeenth century

IN seventeenth-century England, fowling was still largely pursued as a means of filling the pot, and for this purpose, heavy, long-barrelled fowling pieces were used. For country-men and professional wildfowlers it was still mainly a matter of approaching as near as possible to the largest group of birds they could find. That way, they increased their chances of success with the least cost in terms of powder and shot. This form of fowling continued throughout the century, but the restoration of the Monarchy in 1660 saw the beginnings of shooting as a sport: King Charles II and his courtiers had acquired a taste for the fashionable sport of shooting flying birds during their exile in France.

We can get a very good picture of general fowling from a book by Gervase Markham, published in 1621, called *Hunger's prevention, or the whole art of fowling by water and land*. The title suggests that the emphasis was still on fowling as a means of getting food rather than as a sport. Some parts read more like a poacher's handbook, such as his method of taking birds by getting them drunk with a mixture of lettuce, poppy, henbane, hemlock and wheat, boiled up in the dregs of wine. After dealing with various ways of taking fowl by nets, snares and bird lime, Markham discusses shooting and suggests that the best fowling-piece should be about five-and-a-half to six feet long with a bore a little smaller than that of the military arquebus, somewhere around 16 bore (.662 of an inch). There is, however, evidence that bores as small as 20 were being used for fowling at this period. When treating the question of the size of shot, Markham says that it should not be too large, as the pattern would be too open, or too small, as then it would not have the weight to kill. He advises shooting with the wind where possible, and also behind or to the side of the fowl rather than in front of it; this curious advice suggests a lack of striking energy in the shot. The reason he chose the very long barrel was that, apart from keeping the shot clustered better, it would allow full thrust from the slow burning powder to be developed.

Markham suggests that fowlers make use of all available

9

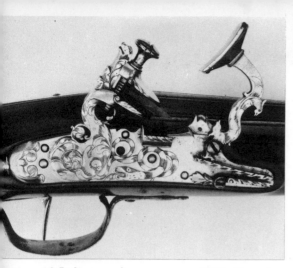

10 Italian snaphaunce gun *c.* 1675. Note the steel from which the sparks are struck and the pan cover are separate

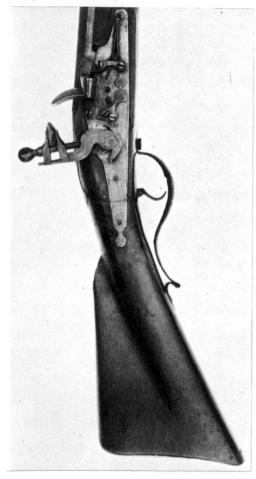

11 English wildfowl gun, *c.* 1650, with earliest form of flintlock, long barrel with hinged support. Note the steel and the pan cover are here combined

cover; hedges, banks and trees. He even advocates the good old stalking horse: any old jade would do, as long as it was well trained and quiet; failing that, a stuffed or pasteboard horse would be satisfactory if it closely resembled a real horse. He mentions that if the fowler should use a bunch of rushes as a screen he should move very slowly since birds are not accustomed to seeing rushes moving about. Dogs, he assures us, should be at heel and under firm control; they should not move after a shot has been fired until commanded. Many sportsmen through the centuries would have derived greater pleasure from shooting if they had heeded Markham's advice and trained their dogs properly.

An early form of flintlock had appeared in Europe in the latter half of the sixteenth century, called a snaphaunce. The name is said to have been derived from a Dutch word meaning a pecking hen, which well describes the action. The flint is gripped securely in the jaws of the cock and, when released, strikes sparks from a steel held in position by the tension of a spring. The cock is connected to the tumbler which, in turn, is connected to the flash pan cover in such a way that when the cock is released the tumbler pushes the flash pan cover open, thus exposing the priming powder to the spark [figure 10].

There is some evidence that the snaphaunce lock originated in Scandinavia around the middle of the sixteenth century; they were also being produced in Nuremberg about that time. This type of lock soon spread throughout Europe: in some countries, notably Italy, fine, richly chiselled varieties of the lock could be found in the seventeenth century.

These snaphaunce locks, though popular in parts of the continent until the eighteenth century, were not widely used in England. In Scotland, however, a curious form of the lock was used on a strange type of gun with a fluted, curved butt. The gun had a lock with an external sear which engaged the rear of the cock and a small ball trigger usually without a guard: altogether, it looked like a gun of an earlier date.

The absence of snaphaunce locks in England was partly due to the fact that the English or dog lock came into use in the first quarter of the seventeenth century. This lock combines the steel with the pan cover in an L-shape, and is held in place by an external spring. When the cock, with the flint in its jaws, is released, it strikes the steel and creates the spark; at the same time the steel is knocked back and exposes the priming to the spark. The name, dog lock, was derived

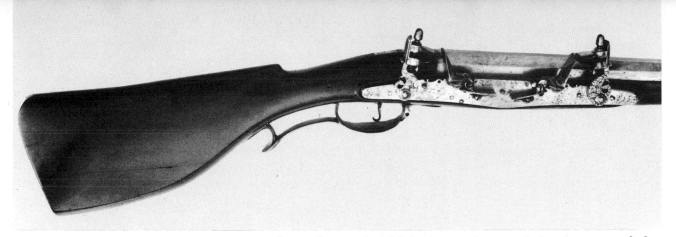

12 French double shot gun by Clulot a Poul.
Designed to take superimposed loads, firing
with single trigger action c. 1645

from the catch which engaged a notch in the rear of the
cock when it was set at safe, or half-cock. These early English flintlocks were strong and robust but rather lacking in
refinement [figures 11 and 13].

In 1634, the Duke of Bedford obtained a Royal Charter
to drain the fens, thus threatening the wildfowlers' liveli-
hood. Their cause was championed by a Mr Cromwell who
was soon to play a leading role on a larger stage.

There are interesting references during the Civil War to
sniping by keepers and huntsmen with 'screwed guns' —
probably screw-barrel flintlock rifles — and fowlers with
long-barrelled pieces. These men had a considerable nui-
sance value since their guns were more accurate than those
used in the armies.

The established order in the countryside changed drastic-
ally. With the general upheaval of the Civil War and sub-
sequently under Oliver Cromwell, large estates were broken
up, deer parks were much reduced, and forests and woods
were exploited to provide timber for various purposes, especially for building ships. In addition the smaller game had
been decimated during the war. When King Charles II was
restored to the throne in 1660, landowners had their lands
returned to them, but had to devote so much of their in-
comes to setting their estates in order again, that the practice
of preserving and hunting deer or maintaining falcons had
to wait. They were content to hunt the hare, and to a lesser
extent the fox; and thanks to the new lighter type of fowling
piece they were able to enjoy the growing and fashionable
sport of shooting flying birds.

At first the new lighter fowling pieces were mostly of
good French [figure 12] or Italian workmanship, but as the
fashion grew and demand for such guns increased, large
numbers were imported from the continent, many of which

13 English breech-loading flintlock rifle
showing Dog-lock

14 Gunmakers Company View and Proof marks on English wildfowl gun, *c.* 1650

15 Double flint over and under gun with swivel breech by Harman Barne, London *c.* 1655 (Most guns of this time were single barrelled)

were more suitable as wall decorations than for hard service in the field. In the year 1667, Mr Pepys recounts in his celebrated diary that, having purchased a French gun, he took it to the Bull Head Tavern to show it off; there he asked the gunsmith Truelock his opinion of it. Edmund Truelock — well named, for he was in fact one of the best London gunmakers of his day — gave Pepys a full account of its mysteries, advising him that it had not been proof fired and was not therefore a gun that could be used with much safety. It seems, however, that Pepys was not much of a country man and did not intend putting his gun to use, and he expressed himself much satisfied with his new, intriguing and decorative piece.

As a result of the many accidents caused by badly made guns, a charter was granted by Charles I in 1637 establishing the Gunmakers' Company of London, with powers to require guns to be submitted for proof before being sold. These powers were strengthened from time to time; one such occasion was at the time of the restoration of Charles II when large numbers of guns of varying quality were being imported.

Barrels were proved by loading them with much heavier charges than normal; if they did not burst in the process, they were examined for any signs of weaknesses such as a bulge, rivel or other visible flaw.

The barrels passed as sound were struck with the marks G P under a crown which stood for Gunmakers' Proof, and also a crowned V which meant that it had been viewed. These marks were normally placed on the top left-side flat of the barrel [figure 14].

English gunmakers were not slow to produce fowling pieces of the new type using the French style of flintlock [figures 15 and 18]. These had a single barrel, about three to four feet long, and a stock with a lighter and better shaped butt which fitted neatly into the shoulder and cheek. This helped when aiming at a moving mark and made it possible to shoot a going away bird with a reasonable chance of success. Shooting at a crossing bird was of course another matter entirely, for the delay between pulling the trigger and the arrival of the shot was such that the shot would pass far behind the bird. Unless the gun was swung on well in front of the bird there was little chance of hitting it. There were, no doubt, occasions when a shooter aimed at the front bird of a crossing covey and was surprised to see the rear bird drop.

In Richard Blome's edition of *The Gentleman's Recrea-*

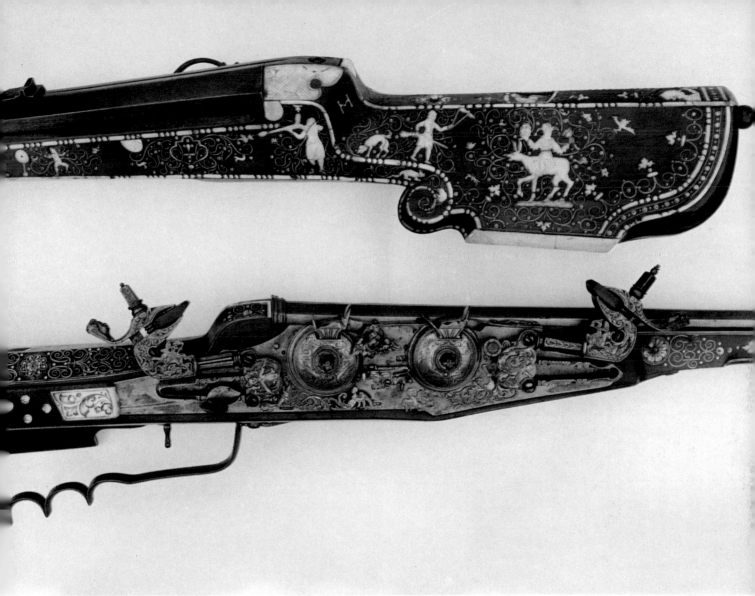

16 (*top*) Match-lock target rifle, south German *c.* 1580; (*above*) German wheel-lock rifle *c.* 1595, firing two shots from one barrel superimposed

tion, published in 1686, there is a section dealing with the new art of shooting flying game, enlivened with some delightful engraved plates which show clearly the current manner of shooting a variety of birds. Shooting from horseback was a popular pastime for gentlemen, with servants in attendance to reload their guns and carry the bag, and dogs to find and retrieve the game [figure 9]. Blome suggests that partridges should be shot as they are going away in flight, but advises a different method of approach for pheasants: having flushed them into the trees with their dogs, shooters should creep up to them and pick them off where they perch. Blome goes on wisely to suggest that shooters should let the dogs retrieve the birds and should make a fuss 13

17 English flintlock wildfowl gun by I. Blankle, London, c. 1680

18 Side plate of English flint gun c. 1665. The function of this plate was to hold the heads of the screws that retained the lock

19 (*opposite*) Stalking and going away shots, engraving from *The Gentleman's Recreation* 1686. Note the great length of the duck guns

over them; the dogs might thus be encouraged to greater effort [figure 25].

Blome recommends a six-foot barrel for shooting such fowl as ducks, herons and geese; these guns would be used mainly for stalking sitting fowl with perhaps an odd shot at going away ducks as they took off. He suggests that in choosing a gun, the barrel should be tested for its smoothness and for its evenness of bore. This was done by pushing a piece of card, cut to the exact size of the muzzle, gently down the barrel with the ramrod. Any tight or loose patches would show up its unevenness; only if the card slid smoothly down could the barrel be said to be well and evenly bored [figure 19].

It should be remembered that, short of unscrewing the breech plug, there was no very satisfactory way of inspecting the inside of the barrel. Presumably shooters did use a kind of hooded lantern and a reflector at the other end to shine a beam of light down the barrel and onto the bore. But it is easy to see how in those long barrels rust pits caused by neglect could easily worsen in the course of time until they became dangerous. This danger was sometimes increased, because a man who was careless about cleaning his gun would probably be equally careless about the quantities of powder and shot he used in loading. A dirty touch hole could cause the gun to miss or hang fire; while a dirty barrel could cause excessive recoil.

Blome states that the ideal flintlock is one in which the mainspring is so well matched with the spring holding the combined steel and pan cover that, when the flint sweeps down the steel (which should be of the correct hardness), the spark is struck just at the moment the priming is exposed. This shows that many of the ideal qualities of a flintlock were understood even then. However, it was not until the early years of the nineteenth century that the flintlock was finally perfected [figure 17].

Blome recommends walnut or ash for making stocks, though the finest and most ornamental ones are to be made from maple. In fact, root maple was popular at this period for its very attractive grain, but it went out of fashion because of its brittleness and its liability to crack. The walnut Blome refers to is the English walnut, but, although strong and sturdy, it has an unattractive grain. Finely figured walnut stocks were imported from Europe.

He encourages the new style of shooting fowl in the air for the reason that a bird on the wing has a larger part of

20 German wheel-lock rifle by Hans Heller dated 1671

its body exposed. But, Blome is curiously in error on the subject of shooting crossing birds: he says that, although some people think one should aim ahead, he thought that the speed of the shot is so great that no allowance is necessary.

It is often supposed that these long-barrelled guns were particularly unwieldy in use, but provided they were of a good weight and balance, they could be swung on to almost any target with reasonable ease; they also had the great advantage of accuracy of alignment, as any error in aiming was at once apparent. The long barrel was still necessary since it allowed maximum propulsion from what was still relatively slow-burning gunpowder.

These long guns must, however, have been awkward to

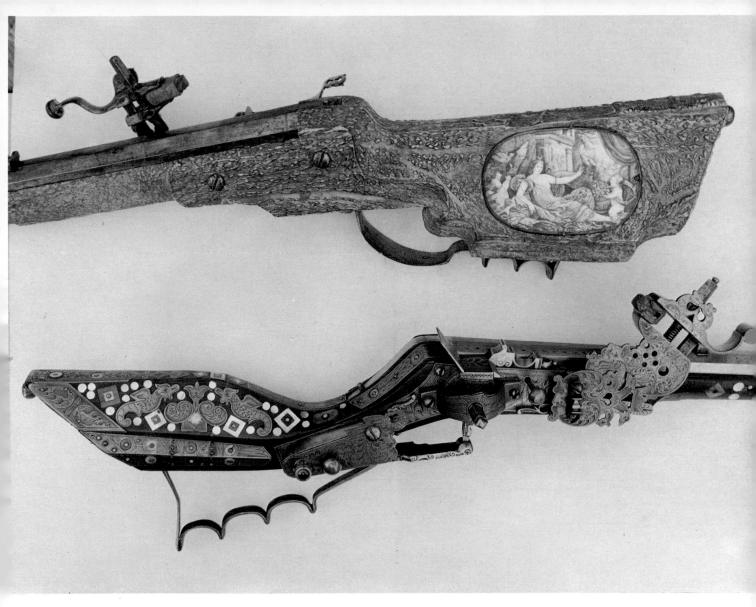

handle in woods, and to reload. They had to be held in an upright position to pour in the powder and shot, and to ensure that the load lay square to the bore.

A long-barrelled, but lighter, better balanced, and more graceful fowling piece for shooting flying birds had come into general use throughout most of Europe in the seventeenth century. Different versions of the French-style flintlock were used [figure 23]. However, a new type of flintlock, known generally as the *miquelet*, had been developed in Spain. This was a strong, angular looking lock with an external mainspring, and an upright cock whose toe-like projection engages the sear. The *miquelet* spread across North Africa, as far as Turkey and the Caucasus [figure 22].

17

It was, however, the Spanish barrels that caught Europe's attention and they were much sought after in the eighteenth century, especially by the English, the French and the Germans. These barrels were usually octagonal in shape for the first third of their length and round for the remainder, with chiselled decoration connecting the two sections. Over the

22 Spanish sporting gun with Miquelet lock by Diego Alvarez, Madrid *c.* 1780

23 French flintlock sporting gun by Piraube aux Galeries a Paris dated 1693

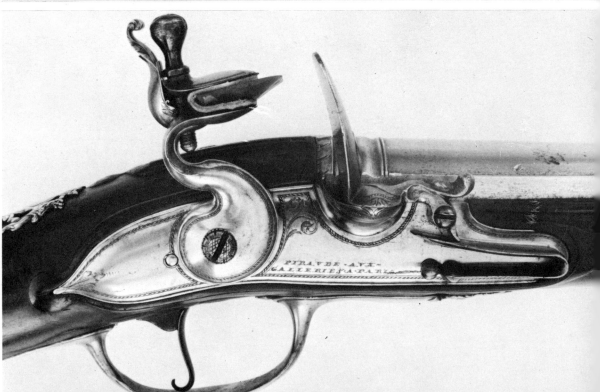

24 Spanish barrel by Nicholas Bis, showing marks on the barrel, *c.* 1715

breech the barrels were stamped with the maker's name, mark and, sometimes, the date and town of manufacture with a gold inset. The particular quality of these barrels lay in the high quality of the iron used and the careful forging, boring and filing. It was said that the iron from which the barrels were made came from the shoes and nails of horses and mules and gained a special quality from being pounded for many miles on the roads. This colourful tale undoubtedly caught people's imagination and helped to sell the barrels. Any hardness gained in road work was removed during the fusing together of the metal at white heat, and subsequent forging and fire welding, but when the barrel was thor-

25 Perching the pheasant and shooting from behind a screen, engraving from *The Gentleman's Recreation* 1686

26 German wheel-lock rifle by Hans Heller dated 1671 reverse side

oughly cold hammered after welding, the metal was condensed and its toughness restored until it had the resilience and strength necessary in a high quality barrel.

Such high prices were paid for the work of the best Spanish barrel makers, notably Nicholas Bis, that forgeries were not uncommon; at any rate, the general style and shape of these barrels was widely copied in the eighteenth century [figure 24].

Alonso Martinez de Espinar gives a great deal of information about gun-making methods in his treatise on guns of 1644; it is remarkable for its detail at a time when production techniques were usually closely guarded secrets. Of particular interest is his comment on the shooting qualities of shot-gun barrels; he writes that it is neither the length nor the weight that makes a barrel shoot well, but the way it is bored. This is the craftsman's secret, though he admits that even the craftsman cannot be sure how a barrel will shoot until it is tested. For no apparent reason some shoot well, and others shoot badly (i.e. scatter widely or unevenly). How to make a barrel shoot well was to remain something of a mystery until the advent of choke boring in the 1870s. Before that date, indeed, from Espinar's time it was found that slightly opening the muzzle end for the last six to eight inches was likely to produce a closer distribution of shot. It was not possible to reduce the art of barrel making to a precise science: it may be easy to recognize the hand of the master, but the intuitive touch, improved with the experience of years, is not easily explained. The great strength of eighteenth-century Spanish barrels, apart from the fine quality of their iron, was largely due to the forging method described in detail by the Madrid gunmaker Isidro Solér in his account of gunmaking of 1795. In the seventeenth century barrels had been made by forging a bar of prepared iron to the required length, and then forging and bending this until the sides met. After this the seam was welded at white heat by hammering it against a hardened rod or mandril inserted inside.

In the eighteenth century a system was devised in which the barrel was forged in a number of separate lengths. The iron for each length could then be separately prepared to the required thickness, so that the grain of the iron would (when the pieces were forged into cylinders) go round the barrel and not lengthwise as before. This, of course, meant that the barrel could stand much greater lateral stress. The weld itself was made stronger by overlapping the iron and forg-

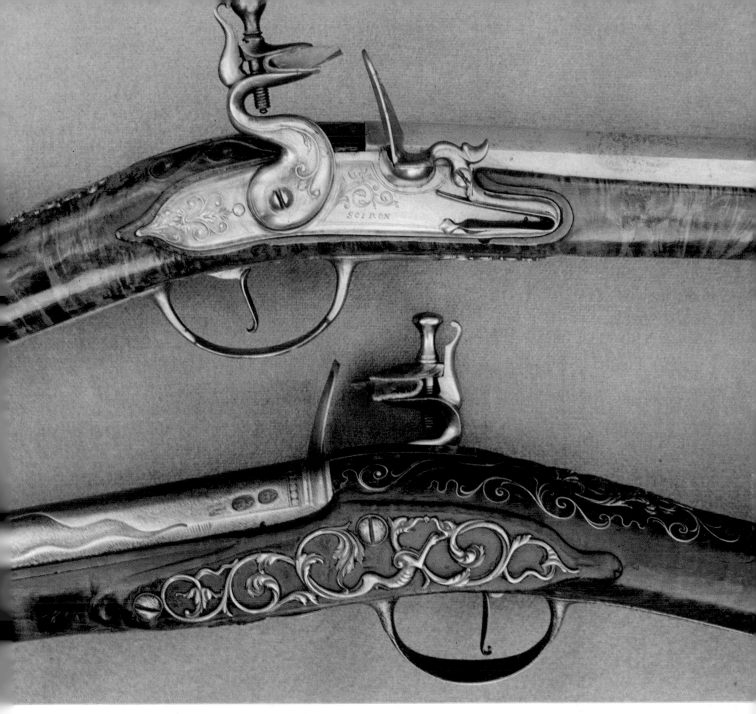

27 (*above*) Gun by Soiron, French *c.* 1685
(*below*) Gun by Bleiberg, London *c.* 1695

ing it to an even thickness on a mandril. The separate
cylinders were then joined by opening the end of one,
inserting the other, and welding them together over a
mandril inserted through both cylinders. The whole barrel
was then thoroughly hammered. As a result, it was a very
strong and durable piece of work which proved superior in
a series of severe tests against other European barrels.

22

Eighteenth Century

28 Sporting gun with silver mounts by H. Delany, London *c.* 1730, with Spanish barrel by Nicholas Bis, *c.* 1720

THE beginning of the eighteenth century saw game shooting as a sport firmly established throughout Europe amongst the landed gentry. Though in some countries shoots took place on a large scale in highly organized parties, in Britain the sport was taken in a more leisurely manner. The British sportsman would go out shooting either alone or with friends, taking as much pleasure in being out in the fresh air and working his dogs as in the actual shooting, and he was generally content to bag no more than he could carry.

Some idea of the fashionable image of the sporting land-owner can be gained from the large number of portraits of the country squire in shooting habit, with his shot-belt round him and his fowling piece held so that it could be clearly seen. Other details might include his favourite dogs gazing affectionately at him, and woods and meadows in the background.

In 1727, a small book entitled *Pteryplegia: or, the art of shooting flying* was published. It was by a Mr Markland and took the form of a long poem. Small though this book is, the highly condensed nature of its verse enables it to encompass almost every aspect of shooting at this time. It follows the best traditions of eighteenth-century thought in combining a philosophical approach with practical understanding [figure 32].

Having first taken to task those who prefer to hug the fireside than brave the elements, he describes how a sports-man must clothe himself if he is to be free to mount and swing his gun: he should dress lightly and forego such fashionable encumbrances as high-heels and long lace cuffs. On the subject of loading the gun he wisely counsels the sportsman not to load the gun the night before since the prim-ing powder might absorb moisture and misfire as a result. He suggests that the powder should be well dried in an oven and corked up in a bottle until needed; necessary equipment should include a powder flask, whose cap would serve as a measure, shot of various sizes in a shot-belt round the waist, wadding of compressed tow from an old saddle, spare flints and a turnscrew. Markland adds a flask of brandy to the

29 Engraving from *Abbildungen der Jagbaren Thiere* by Johann Elias Ridinger, Augsburg 1740

31 Gun by Diego Esquibel, Madrid 1724 and contemporary powder flask

shooter's list to fortify him if his spirits should flag, but warns him that if he drinks too much, not only will his shooting suffer, but he might also kill his own livestock.

Turning to loading, Markland advises four parts of lead shot to three parts of powder; the powder should be well rammed with a thick wad of tow, and the shot lightly rammed with a smaller wad: the pan should not be over-filled with priming powder for it would be compressed when the pan cover was closed and this could cause the gun to hang fire and thus distort the aim. Because of the long barrel it was not practicable to carry the gun barrel downwards,

30 (*above*) Gun by Bleiberg, London *c.* 1695
(*below*) Gun by Soiron, French *c.* 1685

especially as any mud in the muzzle could cause the end of the barrel to be blown off; Markland therefore counselled the safe shooter to carry his piece barrel upwards, with thumb on the cock as an extra precaution. The excellent practice of immediate reloading is mentioned: when the gun has just been fired the barrel is still hot and dry, and the residue of the powder has not had time to absorb moisture from the air.

When it comes to shooting, it is interesting to note that Markland discourages firing at close, overhead, or crossing birds: he rightly suggests that they should be allowed to fly

25

on until they become almost going away shots, thereby increasing the chance of success, also the spread of the shot is wider at a distance.

We shall conclude with two little pieces, in delightful verse, which show both his style and his excellent advice:

> There sprung a single Partridge – ha! she's gone!
> Oh! Sir, you'd Time enough, you shot too soon;
> Scarce twenty Yards in open Sight! – for Shame!
> Y'had shattered her to Pieces with right Aim!
> Full forty Yards permit the Bird to go,
> The spreading Gun will surer Mischief sow;
> But when too near the flying Object is,
> You certainly will mangle it or miss.

Markland could not bear to see a man put drinking and eating before his sport, as the following passage suggests:

> Else each who does the Glass unwisely take
> E'er Noon a false and Fatal step will make;
> The first will Turkeys slay, and make Pigs squeak,
> The latter, ten to one, will break his Neck.
> Yet how my Blood's on fire! oh! how I hate
> I' th' midst of Sport to see a Glutton eat,
> When Pheasants mount, and the Gay Birds arise,
> To see a Coxcomb paring of his Cheese!
> Scourge, Beadle, from the Fields that cramming Fool,
> Or pack the Mouncher back to School.

Although there was some refinement, the overall shape and mechanical details of shotguns remained much the same during the first half of the eighteenth century. During this time English gunmakers had reached the stage where they were able to build first-rate guns, neat and well finished [figure 28].

32 Shooter with dog. Engraving from the front of *Pteryphlegia* 1727 by George Markland

33 Silver wire decoration on English gun by James Lowe 1765, top view

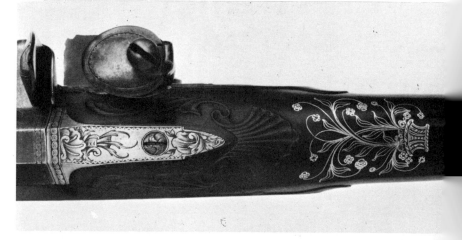

34 Decoration in silver wire on stock of silver mounted gun by H. Delany, London c. 1730

In the second half of the century a number of improvements were made to the lock: the pan was made reasonably waterproof by fitting the pan cover over it in a recessed manner; at the same time the metal around the pan was cut away to allow the water to drain off. The ease with which the pan cover could be flicked forward by the action of the flint on the steel was enhanced by the addition of a small wheel-bearing; and the friction of the mainspring with the tumbler of the lock was eliminated by the use of a small steel swivel between them.

Many of the early and middle eighteenth-century English guns were fitted with Spanish or Italian barrels, but around the middle of the century barrels were being made from strips of iron, forged from a welded mass of horse-shoe nails; these were coiled, edge to edge, in a spiral round a mandril, fire welded and hammered into a strong and resilient barrel. Because the grain of the wrought iron went round the barrel, they were, like the Spanish barrels, much stronger and better able to bear the lateral stress of the explosive force of the powder.

In addition to graceful lines, the English mid-eighteenth-century fowling piece had an elegance of ornament which enriched the gun without detracting from its clean, functional lines [figure 34]. Silver was popular for furnishing the finely shaped heel plates, the richly moulded and chased side plates to hold the lock screws, and the elaborate escutcheons on top of the grip. The stock behind the barrel tang was often finished in a stylized shell design, and, typical of the more decorative examples, was the use of silver wire inlay on the stock, in delicate traceries of intricate curves and curls; this was sometimes supported by a solid inlay of

35 Powder flask c. 1700

27

36 Pair of German sporting guns by I. P. Wilterman a Giessen barrels by Esquibel, Madrid 1727

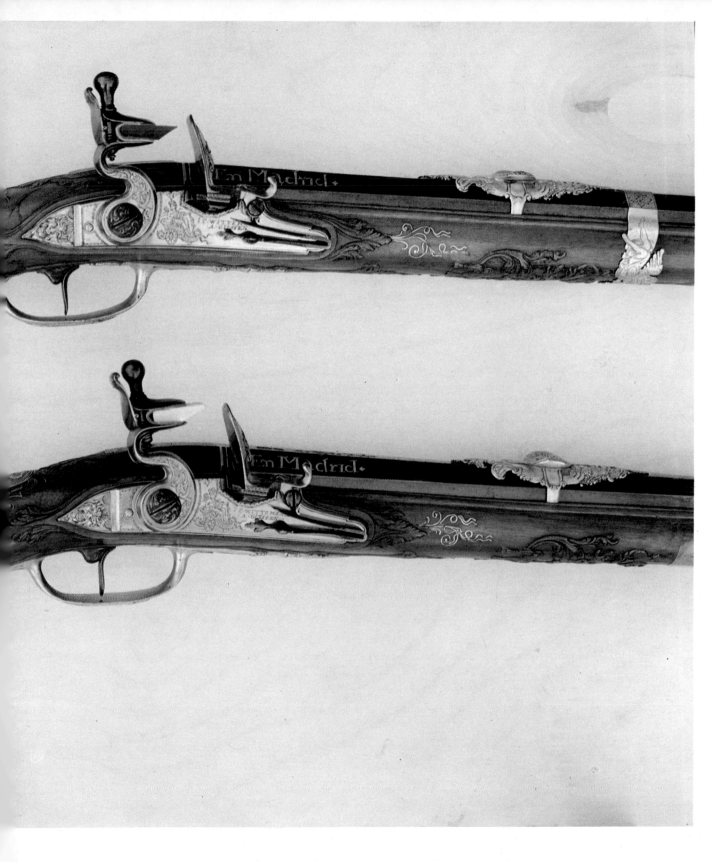

37 Four bore big game rifle by Mortimer, London showing German style patch box and octagonal barrel

flowers and even by hunting scenes or Chinoiserie [figures 35 and 40]. In the early eighteenth century the fore-end of the trigger guard was finished with a foliated trefoil; in time, this took a more solid form, and, by 1750, had changed into the compact acorn shape; this, in turn, gave place to the pineapple before the end of the century.

On the continent, notably in France, Italy and Germany, it was customary to decorate guns in a much more elaborate fashion than in England. In many cases the stocks were ornately carved and inlaid with silver and gold, the locks and furniture chiselled and moulded with a variety of extravagant designs, and the barrels inlaid with gold or chased with ornament [figure 41].

Many more double-barrelled guns were being made in Europe, particularly in France, by the middle of the eighteenth century, but even those with a relatively small bore were very broad across the locks and breeches, and had an unbalanced appearance. More double guns were made in England in the second half of the eighteenth century, but even so they did not become really popular until the turn of the century, when improved powder and Nock's patent breech made thirty-inch barrels practicable.

In this period, the rifle reached its highest point of development in Germany. In the seventeenth century the wheel-lock rifle, with its butt that rested against the cheek, had been almost perfected. It was a popular gun and was used well into the eighteenth century: eventually it was superseded by the 'Jäger' rifle, which was to have a considerable influence on rifle design both in Europe and America [figure 48].

The typical Jäger rifle had a heavy, octagonal, large-bore barrel with multi-groove rifling; its butt was designed to rest against the shoulder though it retained the cheek piece; and the flintlock replaced the wheel lock. There was a patch-box in the butt opposite the cheek piece which closed by means of a wooden slide, and which was large enough to

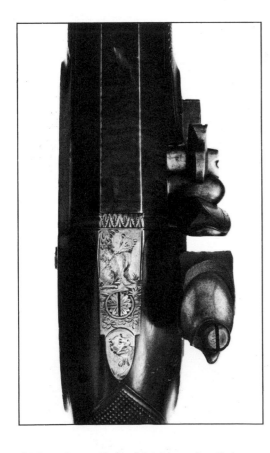

38 Four bore rifle by Mortimer, detail showing top of breech, with engraving of a bear

carry such items as spare flints, a pricker (for cleaning the touch hole), and a turnscrew [figure 37].

An iron ramrod was used because it was customary, in loading, to hammer the bullet tightly down with a mallet. These rifles were normally fitted with finely adjustable triggers and a set trigger mechanism so that they could be fired with great accuracy. This involved setting a spring device which flicked up the sear at the slightest squeeze of the trigger; and so helped to avoid pulling the gun off the point of aim.

These rifles were ideal for the forest and mountain hunting for which they had been designed: they were very accurate and shot heavy balls, both of which features were essential if, for example, deer or wild boar were to be killed outright to prevent the difficulty of recovery if only wounded. By comparison, speed of loading was unimportant.

Modified forms of the Jäger rifle were made by most European countries in the latter half of the eighteenth century to hunt the larger European animals and, less frequently, the big game of India and Africa. Immigrant Swiss and German gunmakers who settled in Eastern Pennsylvania introduced the Jäger rifle to America. This was eventually adapted to the so-called Kentucky rifle, which was used by the early frontiersmen and trappers [figure 43].

These Kentucky rifles were designed to meet the needs of the frontier, and in wild country were equally suitable for hunting or self protection: they had a smaller bore of between .4 and .5 of an inch and a longer barrel of between forty and fifty inches. The smaller bore enabled a man travelling light to carry more balls at the same weight; the increased length of the barrel was probably necessary because a slower burning powder was used in America; moreover,

39 English flintlock sporting gun, one of a pair, silver mounted by Griffin, London 1779

40 Silver wire decoration on English gun by James Lowe 1765, side view

31

41 Pair of German sporting guns by I. P. Wilterman a Giessen barrels by Esquibel, Madrid 1727, showing side plates and richly decorated stocks

42 (*opposite*) Sportsman with dog and gun in eighteenth century costume. Staffordshire porcelain mid-nineteenth century

the bullet was less tightly rammed than in the Jäger rifle.

The use of a slower burning powder in a long barrel could account for the renowned accuracy and relatively low trajectory of these rifles. It is well known that if a ball, keyed into the rifling by means of a cloth or leather patch, is to be easily rammed home, the thrust from a fast burning powder must not be too sudden nor the load too large or the ball will strip across the rifling and lose its accuracy. There is no doubt that the relatively slow but even thrust of a coarse powder down a long barrel avoided this: the rifling was held and the ball achieved its greatest velocity as it left the muzzle. The long barrel did not improve the rifle's accuracy but helped the shooter make an accurate sighting, and the barrel's considerable weight gave added steadiness to the aim.

These rifles had full stocks in ripple grained maple though some were finished with a tiger striped effect; this was achieved by binding the stock with tarred hemp cord which blackened the wood in stripes when it was burnt. The butt had a pronounced bend and the heel plate was of concave shape to fit round the shoulder. The butt also contained a

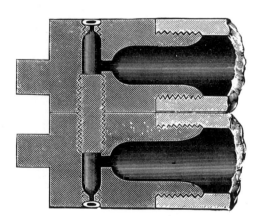

large, hinged brass patch-box on the off side, often finished very decoratively [figure 47]. The locks for these rifles were mostly imported from Germany or from Birmingham in England. Their slim elegance, shooting qualities and, not least, their associations with the frontier heroes of the past make these rifles favourite collectors' items, particularly in America.

To return to the English shotgun of the latter part of the eighteenth century, it has already been mentioned that the shortening of barrels had become possible, not only because

44 Henry Nock's Patent Breech. Woodcut, 1787

45 (*right*) English powder horn with silver mounts, *c.* 1760.

of the better quality powder available, but also because of the invention by Henry Nock in 1787 of patent breeching [figure 44]. By this invention the initial explosion in the breech blasted a flame through the whole charge, thus causing the full force of the powder to be generated more quickly. In the last twenty years of the eighteenth century, the best type of game gun was a halfstocked shotgun with a pair of thirty or thirty-two-inch barrels; the fore part of the stock was held by a bolt to a loop under the barrels and the bend of the stock was straighter with a chequered grip. Altogether it was a plain, functional gun with graceful lines.

When we look to the nineteenth century, we see the final development of the flintlock gun, the invention of percussion ignition and lastly the final burst of inventive energy that was to transform the breech-loaders of the 1850s into the modern sporting gun.

47 Late Kentucky rifle, percussion with silver mounts, c. 1840

48 Jager flintlock rifle, silver mounted, by
Paul Poser of Prague, *c.* 1750 and a powder
flask

49 (*opposite*) Sportsman with dog and gun —
by or after Ben Marshall, famous painter of
sporting subjects

50 Colonel Hawker and Joseph Manton.
Jollification after partridge shooting at Long-
parish, September 1827

Nineteenth Century

51 Double flint gun by Durs Egg, London
c. 1810. French cocks and rainproof pans

THE English double-barrelled sporting gun, which had reached an advanced stage of development by the end of the eighteenth century, was further improved and refined in the first twenty years of the nineteenth century.

When we consider the final glory of the flint gun the name of Manton at once comes to mind. John Manton set up on his own in 1782, after leaving the celebrated gunmaker, John Twigg. John Twigg was one of the first English gunmakers to build good double guns and Manton learned much of his craft from him. Joseph Manton, John's younger brother, started his career as an apprentice to John and left him in 1789 to start his own business. Both brothers excelled in making fine guns of all types, but Joseph applied his inventive mind particularly to perfecting the double-barrelled sporting gun.

Joseph Manton had a lively nature: he was for ever thinking up something new and patenting his inventions. As a result of his work public interest in the sporting gun was maintained in an age when every sort of robust field sport was practised alike by the highest and the lowest in the land.

A contemporary of Joe Manton was Colonel Peter Hawker, who both immortalized Joe and his guns in writing, and used relentlessly in the field the guns whose virtues he so praised.

Some of Joe Manton's inventions were of interest only to those who were bemused by novelty for its own sake. But they included important improvements which considerably raised the performance of the gun. Amongst these was a method of making the gun fire more rapidly. The cock was strongly sprung and its action made short and sharp; at the same time the touch-hole was closely connected to the main charge by setting in the breech at this point [figures 51 and 53]. The recessed breeches also allowed the locks to be more narrowly set, thus improving the gun's appearance. Joe's patent elevated rib, which caused the shot pattern to throw high of the point of aim, enabled the shooter to keep the birds in view when aiming, since the barrels did not block them from sight. Better aiming, excellent balance, together with

52 Colonel Peter Hawker's favourite Joseph Manton Gun, 'Old Joe' with his shot belt, powder flask and shot chargers, and Hawker's book, *Instructions to young sportsmen*

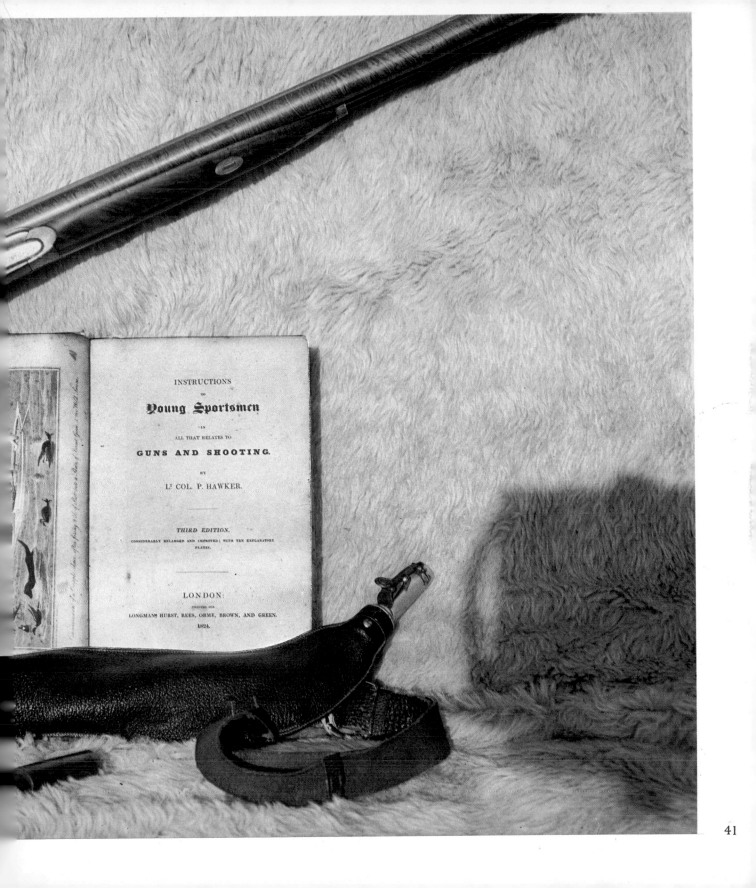

fast, reliable ignition, increased the shooter's chance of success and enhanced Manton's popularity as a gunmaker. In addition, the gravitating stop, which held the cock secure when loading, was one of Joe's most important safety devices.

Both John and Joe Manton took to making touch-holes of platinum between 1805 and 1810, and they also used platinum for the lines and name stamps on the top of the breeches. Many of the flash pans they designed were neat, narrow and cut away to drain off moisture; and Joe also evolved a breech which provided a drain for the water which had run down between the barrels and the elevated rib, to an outlet through the 'pineapple', in front of the trigger guard. Joe and John had a great influence on the sporting gun and within a few years all the best makers were turning out the Manton-type double gun with only slight variations in detail.

Colonel Peter Hawker's best selling book, *Instructions to Young Sportsmen in all that relates to Guns and Shooting*, first published in 1814, ran to many further enlarged editions. This book awakened wider interest in the scientific aspects of gunmaking and stimulated a desire to perform better in the field. Hawker, with his tremendous enthusiasm and his direct manner, set out his thoughts on all matters concerning gunmaking and shooting practice. He made it his business to find out all he could about gunmaking techniques, and put his theories to the test in exhaustive practical trials. The co-operation between Joe Manton and Peter Hawker was very largely responsible for the prominence attained by English gunmaking and for setting the pattern for the development of the sporting gun for the rest of the nineteenth century.

Colonel Hawker lived at Longparish in Hampshire and did much of his shooting on his estate, sometimes straying, in his enthusiasm, over his neighbours' boundaries. He made his particular interest one type of shooting, namely wildfowling, which had largely been left to professionals and locals shooting for the pot. With large punt guns, carriage guns and big bore shoulder guns he waged a full scale offensive against ducks and geese along the coastal saltings. Two of his guns, which must surely be amongst the most celebrated of all sporting guns, are now happily in hands worthy to cherish them. The first of these guns is Hawker's duck gun 'Big Joe', which was made to his specification by Joe Manton in 1814. Its five bore, stub-twist barrel was forged by the famous William Fullerd and its stock was shaped with a pistol grip. The whole gun weighs nineteen pounds and was designed to throw about five ounces of shot. It was later altered to percussion ignition and restocked. The second is Hawker's favourite game gun, 'Old Joe', his first purchase from Joe Manton in 1807. It is a 19 bore gun weighing seven pounds four ounces, which was converted to percussion ignition [figure 52].

A lively engraving in the later editions of Hawker's book shows a scene of jollification after a day's shooting at Long-parish in September 1827. Hawker is mounted on his pony on which he used to gallop to places where partridges were signalled as being marked down. The boy depicted at the rear used to hold the pony while Hawker got off to shoot. Joe Manton stands beside him looking as if he is enjoying himself [figure 50].

The growth of interest in shooting at this time, involving larger numbers of people and the use of more efficient double guns, was accompanied by increased activity in breeding and preserving game. Estates were increasingly bought or let for their shooting, and this inevitably led to the employment of more keepers and sometimes of man-traps, spring-guns and other anti-poaching devices. The method of driving pheasants from woods and copses was occasionally used, but in general shooters walked up their game with the aid of pointers and setters [figure 55].

54 English powder horn with detachable spring top and original silk cord, *c.* 1825

55 Partridge shooting, coloured aquatint from
Annals of Sporting 1822

The sportsman, in addition to carrying the most efficient form of double flintlock gun, now also had powder of excellent quality and shot which was perfectly round and regular in size. Since the last quarter of the eighteenth century shot had been made by the novel method of dropping molten lead through sieves from the top of a high round tower. The lead fell into water which cooled the round shot; it was then graded into various sizes ranging from goose shot to snipe shot.

Flints of the highest quality were needed to make flintlocks operate reliably. The best were deep mined black flints. These were shaped with extraordinary skill especially by the flint-knappers of Brandon in Suffolk where, surprisingly enough, this traditional craft is still pursued today. Their flints are needed for the flint guns which are still in use in remote parts of the world; they also go to the rapidly increasing numbers of collectors of such guns.

In the first years of the nineteenth century it was increasingly the custom for gunmakers to supply their best guns in fine mahogany brass-bound cases, mostly lined with green baize and containing all that a sportsman might require for loading and cleaning his gun [figure 59]. This equipment would usually include a powder flask, a shot-belt, a wad cutter, a wallet for carrying spare flints, a pricker for

56 Pigeon trap shooting showing early method. Coloured aquatint from *Annals of Sporting* 1822

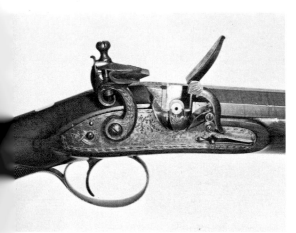

57 Flintlock gun made by John Manton in 1820 for the 6th Duke of Bedford. A good example of the last phase of the flintlock

cleaning out the touch hole, and a turnscrew. For cleaning there were rods, jags, brass 'turks's head' brushes, wool mops, tow and a brush for cleaning the lock. Useful optional items were a spare ramrod a strong double worm for withdrawing wads, and a mainspring clamp used in stripping the lock. The cases for rifles and for some shotguns contained bullet moulds of the ball type. As cases became more common, elaborately engraved trade labels came to be added on the inside of the lid: these sometimes gave interesting information about new patent devices or noble patrons.

While the flintlock gun was being perfected, a rival form of ignition was discovered that eventually ended the long reign of the flint. But this did not come about at once since sportsmen were very attached to the flintlock.

The new development was percussion ignition, made possible by the invention of a detonating powder which exploded on being hammered. Its inventor was the Reverend Alexander John Forsyth, a minister of Belhelvie in Aberdeenshire, Scotland, who patented it in 1807. The original Forsyth percussion ignition involved a small magazine, which from its shape is often referred to as the 'scent bottle'. When turned, this magazine deposited a small quantity of detonating powder into a tube that screwed into the breech and at the same time formed the axis for the magazine; which

45

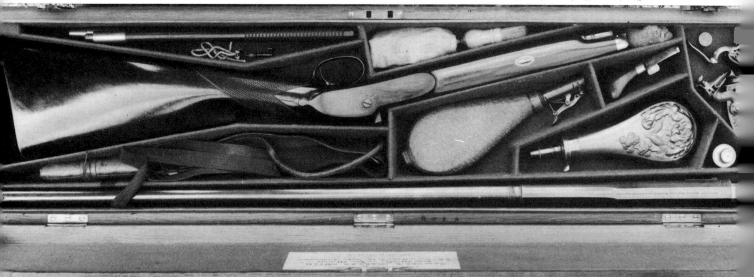

58 James Purdey double flint gun *c.* 1820. Very few flint guns were built by him and most of these were converted to percussion

59 Single barrel flint sporting gun by Samuel and Charles Smith London, *c.* 1820 in original oak case complete with all fittings

was then returned to its upright position. The powder was ignited when the firing pin, fitted with a return spring, was hit by the hammer. The main advantage of percussion ignition lay in its speed, which was very important when firing at a moving target, and it was not long before various ingenious ways of applying the principle were forthcoming from most of the leading gunmakers; they used detonating powder in pills, discs, tubes, tapes and caps. Of these methods, the one to be most widely adopted was the copper cap with anti-corrosive powder inside the top and damp-proofed with tin foil. This cap, fitted over a hollow, cone-shaped nozzle (usually referred to as the 'nipple'), [figure 88] which screwed into the breech. The tube lock continued in limited use especially among pigeon shooters, who considered that its speed and reliability gave them a slight advantage in match shooting [figure 61].

In the 1820s there was still heated controversy about the merits of the flint and the detonator, but by 1830 very few flints were still in use. Many of the flint guns were converted to the new form of ignition: one cheap and popular method was to screw a side plug containing a nipple into the place of the touch-hole, and replace the cock with a percussion type hammer. A superior method involved fitting new breeches and new percussion locks.

One of the factors which helped sway public opinion to

60 Pigeon trapshooting at Hornsey Wood. The trapper pulls one of the five cords to release the bird

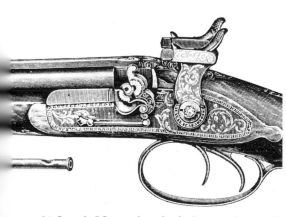

61 Joseph Manton's tube-lock gun, favoured by pigeon shots for its quickness and certainty of ignition

the percussion gun was its superiority over the flintlock in pigeon match shooting [figure 56]. This sport had started in a casual way when the flintlock was still undisputed master but had quickly become highly competitive in nature. It is referred to in the Annals of Sporting of 1822 as a separate branch of gunnery practised by a distinct class of sportsmen, with the perfection of marksmanship and the opportunity for betting as its professed objects. In the early days it often took place on a suitable field close to a public house; the pigeon was placed in a box trap which was pulled open by a cord when the shooter gave the signal. It is said that the famous 'Old Hats' Public House, at Ealing, near London, got its name from the use of hats as makeshift traps, placed over small holes in the ground. The report of a match, in July 1821, records that the winner of the Crinden medal at the 'Old Hats' Club killed only thirty-two out of sixty birds in spite of the fact that percussion guns of enormous dimensions were being used. There was apparently much comment on the impropriety and unsportsmanlike nature of using guns this size, and it was suggested that there should be a return to the ordinary gun carried by gentlemen in pursuit of game. It is interesting to note this use, at that time, of specialized large-bore percussion guns for pigeon shooting. They were single-barrelled guns [figure 62] of from ten to four bore, and can usually be distinguished from wildfowl guns by their shorter barrels, their higher degree

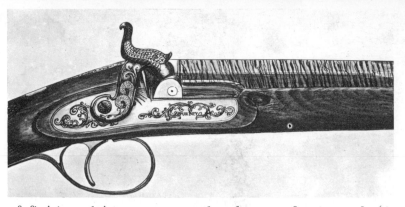

62 Eleven bore percussion cap pigeon gun by J. Purdey *c.* 1823. Number 483, with fine twist barrel by the famous barrel borer Charles Lancaster

of finish and in many cases the absence of a ramrod. (A loading rod was carried in the gun case for this purpose.) In pigeon shooting, where the sportsman had to shoot at a rising bird, a degree of elevation in sighting was desirable, so that the centre of the shot pattern would be high of the point of aim. The Manton type of elevated rib had this advantage, and its adoption by pigeon shooters led to its wider use in game shooting.

In 1822, a time when class distinctions were very wide in England, pigeon shooting was described as being an open sport in which any man might exercise his gun. Pigeon matches became increasingly popular. 'Marksman' in his book *The Dead Shot* refers to prizes of guns, rifles, gold and silver cups and tankards; also to prizes of money, sweepstakes and handicaps and entrance fees for competitors ranging from £1 to £5. Large money prizes and betting unfortunately attracted 'professional' pigeon shooters, who used all the tricks in the book in order to win, such as hiding extra

63 Equipment for sixteen bore Purdey rifle: bullet mould, spruce clipper, patch-cutter, mallet & starter, nipple-key, worm, linen patches and 1 oz. balls

64 (*opposite*) Purdey 15 bore gun cased with fittings 1857
Purdey 16 bore rifle cased with fittings 1851
Purdey 95 bore 2 groove rifle cased with fittings 1865

shot in paper waddings. The rather casual rules under which pigeon matches were conducted all over England were at last standardized when clubs were formed in the 1850s and 60s: these were Hornsey Wood House [figure 60], the Hurlingham, the Orleans and, in 1861, the largest of all, the Gun Club at Notting Hill. Amongst other things their rules established, as the standard pigeon gun, the double-barrelled twelve bore shotgun, firing a load of not more than $1\frac{1}{4}$ ounces.

Pigeon shooting was also very popular on the continent of Europe. The leading French club, whose rules were widely followed, was the 'Cercle des Patineurs' situated in the Bois de Boulogne. But perhaps the most famous meeting ground of all was Monaco, where large numbers of experts from many countries competed for the Grand Prix de Monte Carlo and the Grand Prix du Casino.

Let us now return and discuss the application of the percussion cap to the rifle, which, as we noted earlier, was based on the German Jäger rifle, and indeed was still very similar to it [figure 66]. It had a heavy octagonal barrel with multi-groove rifling, and was designed to fire a patched ball [figure 63]; it had a half stock with a cheek-piece on the near side and a patchbox on the other. This type of rifle used a relatively small charge of powder; too much would have caused the patched bullet to strip across the rifling and lose its accuracy. But when the rifle was correctly loaded, a high trajectory resulted because of the low velocity. Such a rifle was designed for shooting deer at from fifty to one hundred and fifty yards, and for this purpose it was quite adequate.

The sporting rifle, however, which had previously occupied a minor role in Britain received new attention as a result of events at home and abroad. Queen Victoria came to the throne in 1837 and shortly afterwards married Prince Albert. They both loved Scotland, especially Balmoral, and visited it often. Prince Albert was very fond of deerstalking and it was through him that this highland sport became both fahionable and popular. Moreover, the advent of railways made Scotland infinitely more accessible.

As the British Empire spread, soldiers, officials and adventure-seeking explorers, who enjoyed sporting, were provided with undreamed of opportunities for hunting both medium and big game. In India, Ceylon and Africa hunters discovered to their cost that they needed very much more powerful rifles than already existed if they were to stop the charges of elephant, buffalo or rhino. Large rifles of from

65 Chamois hunter with percussion cap, double barrelled rifle

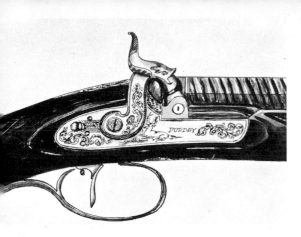

66 Sixteen bore deer rifle by J. Purdey 1851, with deep 10 groove rifling and set trigger, this rifle shoots with great accuracy. The stock is finished to look like ebony

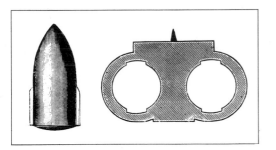

67 The two-groove or Cape rifle showing muzzle and 'winged' bullet

68 Deer stalking in the highlands of Scotland

ten to four bore, had a strong tendency to strip when the ball-gun, but on wide open plains such as those in South Africa, where game was difficult to approach, a rifle was essential. Fortunately a compromise solution was at hand; deep two-groove rifling was used with ball or conical bullets cast with projections that fitted the grooves. These bullets could stand a very high charge of powder without stripping across the barrel. This solution gave reasonable accuracy, a high velocity and a relatively low trajectory, enabling shots to be taken quickly at from fifty to a hundred and fifty yards with only the slightest adjustment in elevation [figure 67].

When hunters came up against dangerous game with a muzzle-loading gun they often needed a quick second shot, so, in preference to relying on a second gun from sometimes unreliable gun bearers, they came more and more to use the double rifle [figures 72 and 83]. This gun represented the height of the rifle maker's art: while it was fairly simple to sight-in a single barrel, it was quite another matter to solder together two barrels which converged at such an angle that bullets from them would hit the same point at one hundred yards. Before and after this point there would be some slight divergence from the centre to right or left, but not enough to matter at normal sporting ranges. If the barrels of a double rifle were exactly set parallel, the right-hand barrel would throw to the right and the left-hand to the left.

The new and unexplored hunting grounds attracted men of tremendous courage and endurance, who were lured on by a love of adventure and sometimes of exploration. Fort-

69 A near go with a tiger – Lieutenant Rice saves his friend. Colour lithograph from *Wild Sports c.* 1870

70 (*opposite top*) 'The Old Shekarry' caught by the rogue elephant. Coloured lithograph from *Wild Sports c.* 1870

unately some were as skilled in the use of the pen as with the rifle, so that we too may now share the wonder and excitement they felt when they saw mighty hordes of animals in places where no European had set foot before, and relive with them the hard-learned lessons of the chase. Among such men were Sir Samuel White Baker, who hunted first in Ceylon and later while exploring Africa; H. A. Leveson, who wrote of hunting in India under the name of the 'Old Shekarry'; William Cotton Oswell, who with Dr Livingstone and Murray explored and hunted northwards from Southern Africa; and Roualeyn George Gordon Cumming, who trekked with his ox waggons northward from the Cape, hunting elephants for their ivory.

These sportsmen all hunted in the days of the muzzle-loader and in consequence had to contend with many problems of which the modern sportsman is happily unaware: the desperate efforts to ram home a sticking ball while a powder load was increased, and without the necessary velocity the heavy ball was useless. The hunter was faced with the choice of using either a smooth bore gun firing a very heavy charge, which would give tremendous velocity but was accurate only up to about fifty yards; or an accurate rifle which could not be relied on to provide the vital 'knock-out' blow to stop a charging animal. As most big game was shot at close range, many sportsmen chose the smooth-bore

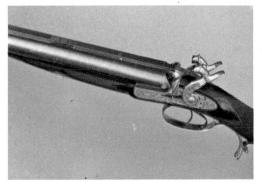

71 (*above and below*) Fine quality double barrelled percussion rifle made in 1863 by Charles Lancaster for the Maharajah of Jodhpur. The locks and furniture are gilded and the Damascus barrels are of the finest quality

wounded buffalo or lion is about to charge; percussion caps that misfire due to having dampened in a sweaty pocket. The dreadful moment of suspense that came after the first barrel had been fired at a charging animal; everything was obscured by the smoke from the large powder charge. There was no time for the hunter to aim a second shot: either the beast was upon him or, to his relief, he could see it stretched before him as the smoke cleared. At the end of the day rifles had to be shot off so that they could be washed through and cleaned in readiness for the next day. A dirty breech might lead to a misfire, and that could cause a man to lose his life.

Baker favoured large-bore rifles of the two-groove type, provided they could stand powerful charges of powder; he was against ball guns because they only had a range of accuracy of about fifty yards. A lifetime's experience in the pursuit of heavy game led him to favour the double-barrelled ten bore rifle, which weighed fifteen pounds and was charged with ten drams of coarse grain powder. He hunted on foot, and shot from distances of a few yards to two or three hundred yards. He brought off very long shots with his single-barrelled two-groove rifle, which weighed twenty-two pounds. It carried a belted ball of three ounces or a conical bullet of four ounces, and had a charge of sixteen drams of powder. This wonderful rifle was made by George

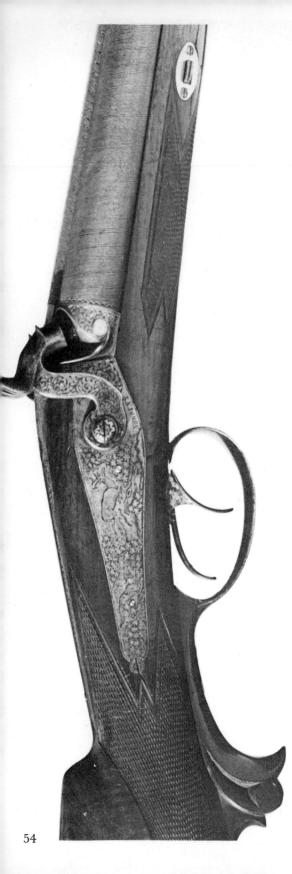

Gibbs of Bristol, and could be relied on to stop the most determined elephant or buffalo charge.

In complete contrast was the hunting method of Oswell, who, in the 1840s in South Africa, pursued his game on horseback, armed with his favourite double-barrelled ten bore ball gun specially made for him by James Purdey of London. With this gun charged with six drams of fine grain powder, he would ride recklessly in pursuit of game across the plains, or through the rough thorn scrub whose thorns eventually clawed away parts of the butt and fore end of the gun's stock. He shot mostly at distances of twenty five yards or less, having run his quarry down or brought it to bay; and, whether elephant, rhino or lion, the ball gun was usually equal to its task. He either dismounted to shoot or shot from the saddle. The great advantage of his gun was that it could be easily loaded while he was in the saddle. The charge was contained in a paper cartridge, and the ball with its waxed on patch could be rammed down the unrifled bore with ease. The most difficult thing he found, was to fit on the percussion caps.

While Oswell tackled his game from the closest possible quarters, such hunters as Gordon Cumming usually fired at seventy or eighty yards and sometimes lay in wait for their quarry at drinking holes. As these distances were beyond the accurate range of a ball gun, powerful big bore rifles were used. There was, however, a type of gun popular in South Africa (sometimes called a Cape rifle) which had one barrel smooth bored for either ball or shot, and the other barrel rifled usually for a two-groove conical bullet or belted ball.

The expression 'Cape rifle' also covered a two-groove rifle of 40 or 42 bore, weighing twelve pounds, and useful for shooting at long ranges on the open veldt [figure 67].

In the days of the muzzle loader the contest between man and beast was more equal; some hunters paid the penalty for rashness or miscalculation by death or frightful injury, while others had extraordinary escapes. Leveson, the 'Old Shekarry', was lucky to survive the following incident while elephant hunting in Southern India. Aiming behind the ear, he fired two quick shots at a bull elephant as it dashed past him: the second shot brought it to its knees but it quickly recovered and regained its feet. The hunter snatched from his bearer his spare gun (a heavy two-ounce double rifle) and ran with all speed along the bed of a dried up stream with high banks on either side, to cut off the elephant's path. On hearing stones clatter behind him, he turned to see the

72 (*opposite*) Double 16 bore rifle by M. Nowotny in Wien *c.* 1850. Fine twist barrels, unusual straight grooves in left barrel, right barrel rifled in normal manner

73 The tables turned, a charge by an African rhino routs the hunters. Woodcut from *Sport in many lands*

74 Samuel White Baker caught at last. Woodcut from his book *The Rifle and Hound in Ceylon*

75 The 'Old Shekarry' buffalo shooting, India. Woodcut from *Sport in many lands*

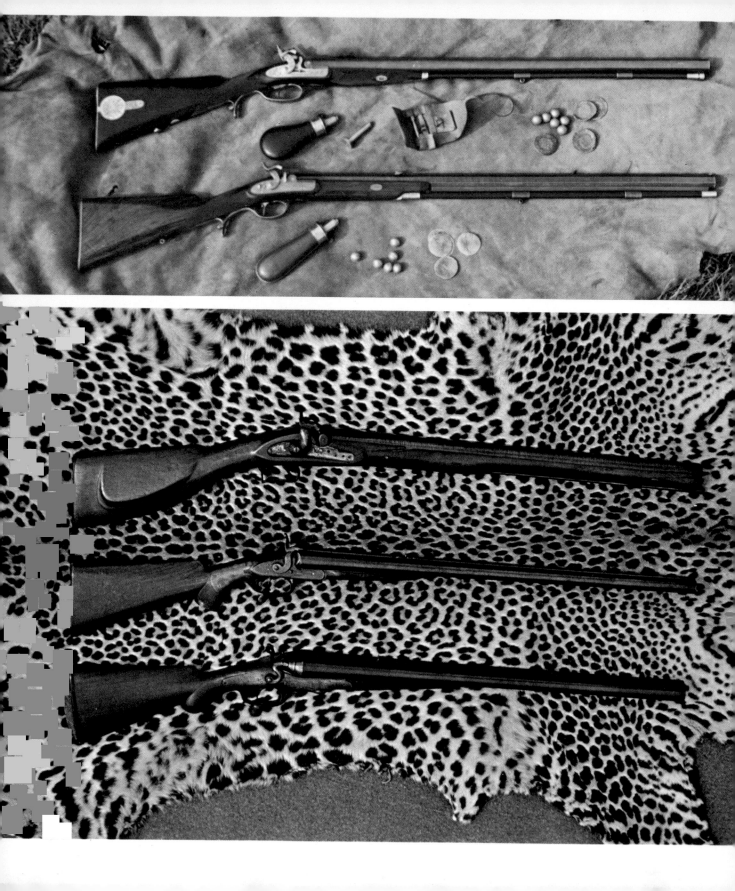

76 (*left*) A double-barrelled percussion 10 bore rifle by Charles Lancaster (1863) and a single barrel percussion, 16 bore, two-groove rifle by Joseph Lang (1853)

77 (*right*) Sportsman in velvet coat with percussion gun and shot flask. A miniature painting, *c.* 1840

78 The 'Old Shekarry' (H. A. Leveson) in a desperate scrape with a black bear. India, *c.* 1840

79 (*left*) Three big game rifles on leopard skin: four bore muzzle-loading elephant gun, ten bore pin fire by Rigby and eight bore hammer gun by Bonehill

infuriated elephant charging down upon him. Since escape was impossible, he knelt on one knee and took steady aim, firing at fifteen yards. But either because he was breathless from his run or because the weight of his rifle was too great, he let his left hand drop. The ball went too low and missed the elephant's brain. Next instant, he was struck by a heavy blow and hurled through the air. When he came round, shaken and bruised, and lying in a pool of blood, he

80 'Feeling both horns of a dilemma'. Oswell caught by two rhinos. Illustration from The Badminton Library: *Big Game Shooting* 1894

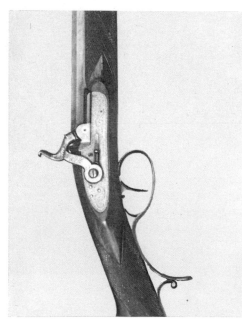

81 Single barrel rifle by J. Purdey 1850, of the type called a rook and rabbit rifle

immediately remembered the danger he was in and retrieved his rifle from the dry bed of the stream below. As he was picking it up, the elephant, which had been pursuing his bearer, turned again towards him and charged. With great difficulty the battered hunter raised his rifle and, taking steady aim between the eyes, fired the remaining loaded barrel. When the smoke cleared the great mass lay before him [figure 70].

Baker too was caught by a rogue elephant which charged suddenly through the long grass with its trunk up. Baker fired but the elephant's trunk prevented a brain shot. He was thrown into the air and landed some yards away. The determined beast threshed the grass with its trunk looking for him and it was lucky for him that the black powder smoke spoiled the elephant's capacity to scent. Baker's leg swelled to twice its normal size, but within a couple of days he was riding out and even dismounting to tackle on foot another rogue which duly fell to his famous four-ounce rifle [figure 74].

Oswell was twice tossed into the air by rhinoceroses [figure 80], once he was on foot, and on the other occasion both he and his horse were tossed up together. He also had a lucky

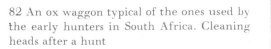

82 An ox waggon typical of the ones used by the early hunters in South Africa. Cleaning heads after a hunt

83 Double barrelled 16 bore deer rifle with extra shot barrels, built by J. Purdey for the 4th Marquess of Bath 1848. One of the collection of family Purdeys at Longleat, Wiltshire

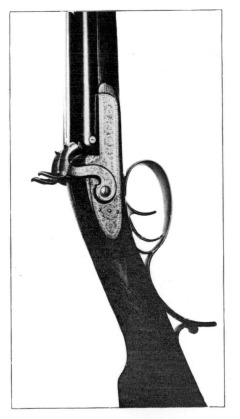

escape when charged by an elephant. He tried to turn his horse in a confined place and fell to the ground, and saw a great foot coming down on his legs. He flung them apart just in time. Incredible though it may seem, the other feet passed over without touching him.

When hunters set out in the middle of the nineteenth century they had to have vast supplies of essential provisions carried in ox-waggons [figure 82]. Here, for example, is a list of some of the items carried by Gordon Cumming's expedition of 1843: numerous guns and rifles, ladles, bullet moulds, loading rods, shot-belts, powder flasks, three hundredweight of lead, fifty pounds of pewter for hardening bullets, ten thousand prepared lead bullets, bags of shot of all sizes, one hundred pounds of fine sporting powder, three hundred pounds of coarse gunpowder, about fifty thousand best percussion caps, greased patches and cloth for making more. In addition to this armament were needed large stocks of food and drink (including the potent 'Cape Smoke' brandy), waggon and harness spares, clothes, tools and trade goods. For the most part they lived off the land and ate large quantities of meat. Oswell said that David Livingstone used to eat four pounds of meat for breakfast on one of their combined hunting and exploring expeditions.

We will leave the last word on big game hunting in this period to William Cotton Oswell, who was described by Sir Samuel White Baker as the greatest of the hunters of southern Africa, the truest friend and the most thorough example of an English gentleman. Looking back in the 1890s to Africa as it was fifty years before, he wrote of his sorrow for the fine old beasts he had killed, admitting that he had been

59

84 Duck shooting, coloured aquatint *c.* 1850

85 (*opposite*) Pair of 15 bore percussion guns built by Charles Lancaster for His Royal Highness Prince Albert in 1843, in fine original mahogany, velvet lined, case. Below, loading rod

young then and there had been excitement in the work; that there had been many men to feed and that the animals had been put to good use. He remembered as the best of companions, Murray, Vardon and Livingstone; and had happy memories of the Africans he had met. He looked back on the free and independent life; the discovery of a new country; how he used to lie beside his waggon at night and look at the stars from a place where no European had been before; and how every patch of bush and every little rise could be all that stood between him and some new, strange sight. The vast herds of animals that stretched as far as the eye could see had now disappeared; farmers, gold seekers and diamond miners had changed the face of the land; houses stood where once he had shot elephants and the railway train would soon be whistling and screaming through all the hunting-grounds south of the Zambesi.

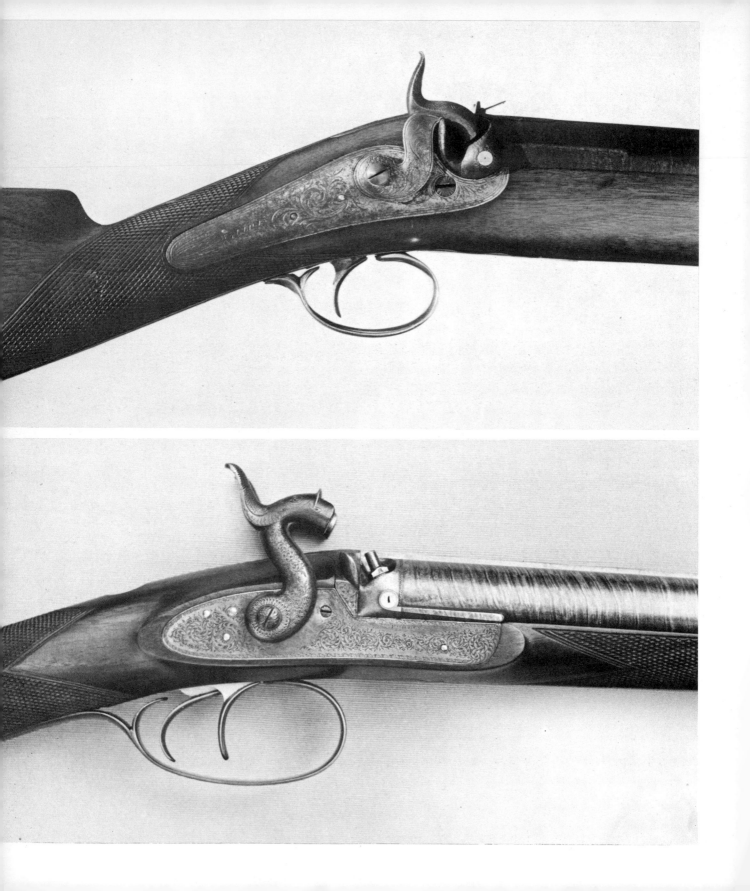

86 (*above*) Baker saved by a charge of six-pences when he had run out of bullets. Woodcut from his book *The Rifle and Hound in Ceylon*

87 (*above left*) Four bore wildfowl gun by Rigby of London and Dublin *c.* 1850 brass furniture 48″ twist barrel 15 lbs. Note leaf sight for long range use

88 (*left*) Fine double 15 bore percussion gun by J. Purdey 1839 Strongly figured Circassian walnut stock. 30 inch twist barrels, weighs 6¼ lbs

To return to a gentler clime, to the dusty autumn stubble and crisp December days when pheasants burst like gay rockets from the coverts, let us look again at Europe where the muzzle-loader was still unchallenged. In Britain, for the most part, game was still walked up with the aid of dogs; but on estates owned by keen shots, the desire for more shooting and larger bags often led to a greater interest in breeding and preserving game birds, especially pheasants. Such books as *Gamonia or the art of preserving game*, published in 1836, helped to stimulate interest in this subject. People began to plant woods and coppices with a view to providing cover for pheasants. They arranged them in such a way that the birds could be easily driven out to the guns. This was a new approach, for in the eighteenth century woods and trees had been planted to conform to a pictorial ideal of classical landscape, and in the early part of the nineteenth century tree planting was aimed to produce a romantic or pictures-que effect.

We have seen how Joseph Manton brought the English sporting gun to a new stage of perfection. However, it was not long before several other makers followed his lead and made improvements on his fine guns; indeed some of the gunmakers who were to spring to prominence had worked

89 Grouse shooting in the Highlands of Scotland *c.* 1850 coloured aquatint

for him. James Purdey, who had left Manton to help Forsyth, started business on his own account at Princes Street, Leicester Square, in 1814; his strong finely finished sporting guns [figure 62], and his early use of the copper cap system brought success and enabled him to take over Joe Manton's premises in Oxford Street in 1826. Charles Lancaster, who had been an excellent barrel borer to the Mantons and other leading gunmakers, was said by Hawker to have

better view, which action probably saved my life, for immediately the brute sprang into the middle of the road, alighting about six feet from the place where I was standing; I fired a hurried shot ere he could gather himself up for another spring, and

90 The Old Shekarry shoots the dreaded man-eater, killer of over 100 persons. Woodcut from *Wild Sports of the World*

allowed many gunmakers to put their names to what was essentially his work. According to Hawker, when Lancaster started business on his own account after Joe Manton's retirement in 1826, he was as good as the best of them when it came to building sporting guns and rifles. Another protégé of Joe Manton was Thomas Boss, founder of the present firm of that name. Of provincial makers, the names of Westley Richards and W. Greener of Birmingham, Gibbs of Bristol, Alexander Henry of Edinburgh and Rigby of Dublin, to name but a few, were noted for their fine work on sporting guns and rifles.

Sportsmen and gunmakers alike believed that the percussion-cap muzzle-loading gun had been perfected and in this they were right: but they were soon to be shaken into a period of tremendous activity, invention and controversy, the intensity of which had never been known before in the whole history of the gun.

The development
of the breech~loader

91 The original Lefaucheux breech-loader, with drop-down barrels, back action locks and big overhead hammers

THE Great Exhibition of 1851 in London, which was inspired by Prince Albert, was destined to be the starting point from which the modern breech-loading gun was eventually developed. It was at the exhibition that Joseph Lang, already well known as a maker of fine sporting guns, perceived the great potential of the breech-loading gun shown there by Lefaucheux, a gunmaker from Paris [figure 91]. As early as 1812, the French gunmaker Pauly had pioneered a type of breech-loading gun with a drop-down barrel; and in 1829 Pottet patented a metal and paper cartridge with a type of percussion cap in the base. The Lefaucheux gun had drop-down barrels, hinged in a similar manner to modern side-by-side guns, which were secured, when closed, by a lever-operated hook which engaged the lump brazed under the breech. It used a paper cartridge with a brass base, which was fired by a brass pin that projected at right angles to it; the other end of the pin connected to an internal percussion cap [figure 93].

This pinfire cartridge had been developed by the Paris gunmaker Houllier in 1850. Although the Lefaucheux gun and Houllier cartridge were fairly crude, they embodied the essential principles on which further development could be based. The cartridge was gas-tight and contained its own means of ignition while the gun had a method of opening and closing that was very simple, and capable of being adapted and improved considerably in the years to follow.

It is much to Lang's credit that within a few months he had built his own improved version of this pinfire gun. Even at this early stage it had an English look about it. Other gunmakers were quick to follow him. In 1852, Charles Lancaster developed the remarkable centre-fire cartridge, to be used in his gun fitted with an extractor. Previously it had been necessary to pull out the spent cases by the pins. The lever used to open and close this gun was swung back over the trigger guard [figure 98].

Bastin Lepage devised a system whereby the barrels were levered to slide forward instead of hinge, but this action proved unsatisfactory [figure 99]. Gunmakers concentrated

92 The Duke in a warm corner. Frontis of W. W. Greener's *The Gun* 1881. Note the girl amid the game

67

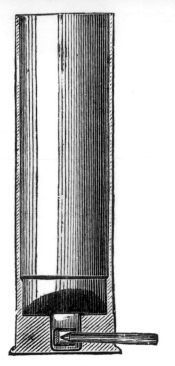

93 Section of the pinfire cartridge case, showing brass pin connecting with the internal percussion cap

94 Barrel boring Birmingham, 1850s. Wood engraving from W. Greener's *Gunnery in 1858*

on improving the pinfire gun with drop-down barrels, and a variety of interesting actions were developed which continued in use into the period of the centre-fire cartridge [figure 101]. There was the Dougal lockfast action in which the barrels were released by a lever and moved forward from the breech face before hinging down. This process was reversed for closure. The Westley Richards gun was closed by a snap action bolt that held the doll's head extension of the barrels to the top of the breech. An early Purdey snap action was activated by a thumb lever through the front of the trigger guard, and the lumps were bolted automatically on closure. Several other actions were invented. But the most popular was the under lever screw action, in which the lump was firmly screwed down by a powerful lever, as it was moved back from the side to its position under the trigger guard [figure 101].

The introduction of these pinfire breech-loaders was welcomed by some sportsmen and bitterly opposed by others. Battles of words with charges and counter charges raged in the sporting magazines until, in 1858 and 1859, Mr Walsh, the editor of *The Field*, arranged trials in which the muzzle-loader was tested against the breech-loading gun. The muzzle-loaders won the day, but on the second occasion only by a narrow margin.

It is interesting to note that the average weight of the breech-loaders was about one pound more than that of the muzzle-loading guns, and generally the powder charge they used was a quarter of a dram greater. However, many considered that the ease and safety of loading and unloading the breech-loader, more than compensated for its slightly inferior shooting qualities.

One of the fiercest opponents of the breech-loader was W. Greener, the Birmingham gunmaker who was celebrated for his application of scientific principles to gunmaking. Having devoted his skills to the improvement of the muzzle-loading gun and rifle, he viewed the newcomer with disdain, and at times spoke of it in thoroughly unscientific terms. In his book *Gunnery in 1858*, Greener sets out his objections in detail. There is no doubt that some of his criticisms of the earliest pinfires were justified. Several early actions were not strong enough to prevent gaping at the breech when the gun was fired, and this defect grew worse with heavy use. The guns were heavier and not as well balanced; they needed more powder to achieve the same result, and thus had a heavier recoil. The round shape of the muzzle-

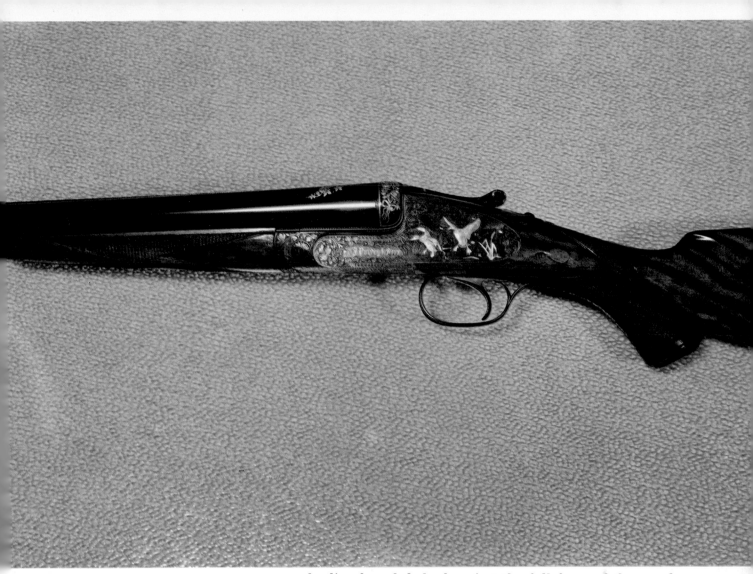

95 Recently built Purdey gun enriched with deep engraving and gold inlay

96 Three strip Damascus coiled, ready for fire welding. A hard steel mandril was inserted inside before welding the white hot iron with hammer blows

loading breech helped project the full force of the powder, unlike the flat face of the breech-loader which resembled the old-fashioned flat breech of the early flintlocks. In addition, gas escaped at the breech and round the pin.

A completely opposite view was taken by H. A. Leveson. He points out the greater safety of loading with the muzzle pointing away, and adds that, with a breech-loader, it was not possible to double load a barrel, nor was there the danger of the powder flask exploding when powder was poured down a barrel in which a piece of tow might be smouldering. The barrels could be easily checked for mud or snow which if the gun were fired could cause the muzzles be blown off, and unloading and cleaning were made extremely simple. Leveson also recalls the annoyance of waiting before the line could move forward, while some old gentleman fumbled in

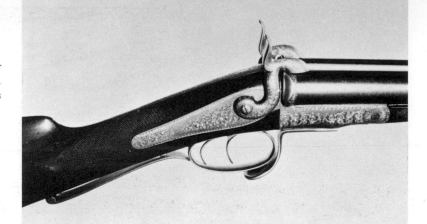

his pockets for wads, caps, powder flask and shot bag. In boggy places it was no longer necessary to put down the butt in the mud when reloading. Leveson goes on to say that no-one who used a breech-loader needed to get raw, blistered fingers from ramming charges home down a fouled barrel, or suffer the difficulty of putting on the caps in bitterly cold weather with numb fingers. He found it an advantage too to be able to change the charge at a moment's notice should a duck appear when the gun was loaded for snipe.

While the tide of argument ebbed and flowed, many sportsmen continued to use their muzzle-loaders, and some even continued to have them made. This was especially the case for pigeon match shooting, percussion muzzle-loaders being made into the 1860s.

The early pinfire guns either used barrels designed for muzzle-loaders or were themselves converted muzzle-loaders. The chamber of the breech was relatively thin in this type of barrel, but when barrels began to be specially forged for breech-loaders they were made thicker at the breech end to allow for chambering; this also allowed for any weakening caused by brazing on the lumps. For extra strength a higher percentage of steel was used in their construction; since these barrels were mainly of the Damascus type [figure 103]. To make them, several alternate bars of iron and steel were welded together to form a square rod, $^3/_8$ inch by $^3/_8$ inch, which was then tightly twisted. Three or more of these were forgewelded together to form a ribbon about three quarters of an inch wide. This was coiled, edge on edge, round a hardened steel mandril, brought to welding temperature and then forged into a solid barrel by being hammered on a U-shaped mandril anvil [figures 96 and 102]. When these barrels had been bored and filed, the beautiful figure of

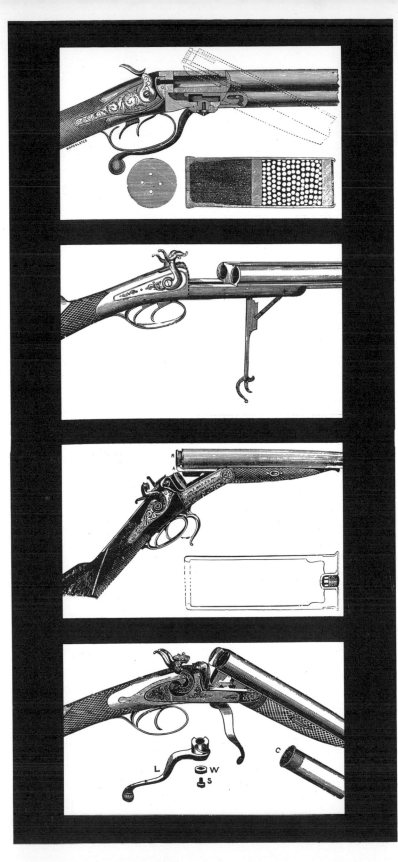

98 Charles Lancaster's centre-fire breech-loader and cartridge, 1852. The detonating mixture was spread across the perforated base in the cartridge

99 Bastin Lepage breech-loader, the sliding breech worked by means of an under lever

100 Daw's centre-fire cartridge and gun, 1861. Note that the cartridge differs little from the present shot gun cartridge

101 Double or screw grip bar-lock gun and centre-fire cartridge. Note the screw on the detached lever

102 Forging Damascus barrels Birmingham 1850s. Wood engraving from W. Greener's *Gunnery in 1858*

103 Types of Damascus. Engraving on copper from W. Greener's *Gunnery in 1858*

104 (*opposite*) Pair of bar-in-wood Purdey guns in original case with fittings 1879, having Damascus barrels and finely figured walnut stocks. Single bar-in-wood Purdey gun 1868 in original case with fittings, including cartridge reloading tools and measures

their alternating iron and steel curves was revealed by process of browning which caused the iron to take on a deep brown hue while the steel remained bright.

These Damascus steel barrels were made in various patterns in many parts of Europe. Those made at Liège in Belgium were particularly renowned for the fineness of their pattern. In England, the Birmingham barrel makers favoured a bolder figure. Without doubt, such barrels are wonderful works of forging artistry and give great character to sporting guns of this period. The best of these are very strong; some, a hundred years old, will go through modern nitro-proof [figure 106].

The pinfire breech-loading gun had only partially eclipsed the muzzle-loader, when in 1861 George Daw introduced into England what was in all essentials the modern sporting centre-fire cartridge. This cartridge, patented in 1855, was the invention of Clement Pottet of Paris and proved to be ideal for use in shotguns. The pinfire cartridge had several disadvantages: not only was it rather awkward for loading, but a corroded pin could stick, and fail to fire the percussion cap. Worst of all, these cartridges were dangerous to carry loose in pockets: they were loaded with black powder, unlike the safe powders of today, and a fall or sharp knock on the pin could explode them.

Soon after the introduction of this cartridge, numerous centre-fire hammer guns were developed which, within a few years, swept aside both the pin-fire gun and the muzzle-loader. No longer was the pin attached to the cartridge as in the pinfire; instead, the centre-fire cartridge was struck by a steel pin or striker that fitted through the standing breech. The hammer that struck the pin was smaller and neater

105 Inside view of rebounding lock, 1868. From 12 bore gun by J. Purdey 1868

106 Centre fire bar-in-wood hammer gun by J. Purdey 1868 under lever snap-action and rebounding locks. This gun shows all original finish

than the big overhead pin-fire hammer. Because of its strength and simplicity, the under lever screw was generally used, especially in large bore guns and rifles.

Some of the early snap actions were improved, but in 1867 the important Purdey bolt was introduced. It had a really secure snap action which was worked by the top lever [figure 107]. Back action locks, in which the mainspring is behind the hammer, had commonly been used for pinfire guns but when central fire arrived some forward action locks were again used. Most important was the rebounding lock, introduced around 1866, in which the hammer rebounded to half-cock and enabled the striker to return behind the breech face. This facilitated the opening and closing of the gun since the hammers did not have to be first raised to half cock; as an added refinement strikers were spring loaded to keep them clear of the breech face, except when struck by the hammer.

There were many forms of the hammer gun, as it is now called; with screw or snap actions, under levers, top levers and side levers; some with back action and others with forward or bar locks; some with the bar in iron and some in wood. The most elegant hammer guns were those with the bar-in-wood extending under the breech right up to the hinge-bolt. Those made by James Purdey are particularly graceful.

The most perfect bar-in-wood hammer guns were being built in the 1870s with beautifully patterned Damascus barrels, top lever Purdey bolt actions, clip-on forends replacing the earlier bolted ones, and with graceful dolphin-headed hammers. The stocks were made from richly grained Circassian walnut, and the locks were decorated with fine, floral engraving. The Westley Richards bar-in-wood gun was interesting in that the stock and the forend covered the hinge-bolt.

Elegantly designed hammer guns were being built by numerous gunmakers: among these, Boss, Grant, Greener, Holland & Holland, Lang, Lancaster, Rigby, Webley and Scott are still well known names today.

W. W. Greener's introduction of his method of choke boring barrels marks the next important development in the hammer gun. This involved boring out the barrel in such a way that the muzzle was left constricted. This prevented the shot spreading too widely. W. W. Greener, whose father so vehemently attacked the breech-loader, brought out his version of choke boring in 1874. He guaranteed that his guns gave a shot pattern at forty yards that was unheard of at that time. This claim attracted wide attention, and so many letters, expressing disbelief were received by *The Field* that Mr Walsh, the editor, arranged another public trial in 1875. Greener's claims were convincingly proved in this

107 Bar-in-wood hammer gun by J. Purdey 1879 showing top lever used with the Purdey bolt and gracefully carved fences

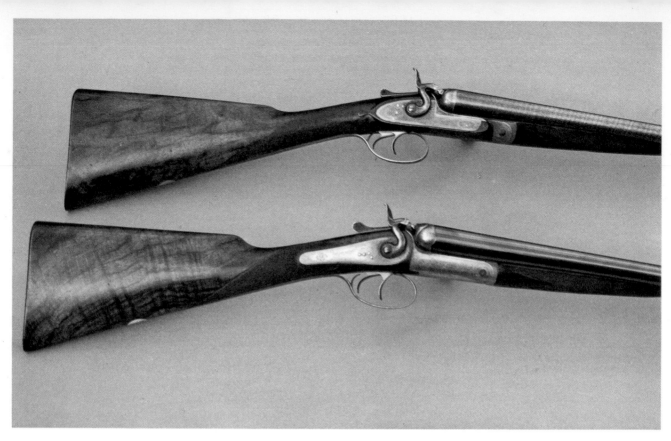

108 (*top*) 12 bore bar-in-wood hammer gun made by James Purdey in 1879 and (*above*) 12 bore hammer gun having back action locks and fitted with ejectors made by James Purdey in 1894 for the Marquess of Ripon

and subsequent pigeon shooting trials at the Gun Club, Notting Hill.

A system of choke boring was also used by Pape of Newcastle, but without doubt it was W. W. Greener who fully exploited and publicised the invention. At last the problem of how to make a barrel shoot close and strong, which had puzzled gunmakers for centuries, was solved. The shooting qualities of the hammer gun of the late 1870s have hardly been improved upon since.

Let us now look again at the sporting scene. In Britain even remote parts of the country were becoming easily accessible due to the spread of railways. It was becoming in creasingly the custom for 'crack' shots to travel long distances for their shooting invited by owners of large estates who competed with their fellows for the largest bag. On some big estates, casual shoots restricted to local sportsmen were being replaced by more highly organized affairs in which large numbers of beaters were involved. Pheasants which had been reared in hundreds earlier in the century, were now being reared by thousands on many estates. It is revealing to note that between 1802 and 1853 Colonel Hawker bagged only 575 pheasants, while Lord Ripon between 1867 and

1895 bagged 111,190. Hawker's 7,035 walked up partridges may be compared with Ripon's 89,401, mostly driven partridges. There is little doubt that Hawker worked just as hard for his smaller bag and with as much satisfaction as Lord Ripon. But he only hunted his own coverts and some of his neighbours', while Lord Ripon shot over the best estates in England and many on the continent. Notable among the later were the fabulous estates in Hungary owned by Baron de Hirsch where prodigious bags could be made.

The extensive rearing and preserving of birds on large estates meant employment for numerous keepers [figure 110], in addition to the small armies of beaters required. Shooting in the grand style thus became a very expensive pastime and reflected an age of wealth and privilege.

The pleasure a sportsman felt at being invited to a fashionable shooting party might have been dampened by

109 Driven grouse, coloured engraving by A. Stuart-Wortley, sportsman and artist. Shooting with hammer guns c. 1880

the fact that his wife was expected to appear in four different costumes every day, one for each breakfast, luncheon, tea and dinner. Moreover, it was not done to wear the same costume twice. On the other hand, twelve new costumes for a three-day shoot presumably made shooting popular with the women. It was customary to change into tweeds at midday and to go and watch the men shooting. Afterwards they would all lunch together in a tent or convenient lodge.

Fashionable shooting house parties of the late Victorian and Edwardian periods were a far cry from the shooting of the first half of the nineteenth century. There were, of course, some who carried on the traditional method of walking up with dogs, and others who followed high fashion at a distance and copied this style of shooting at a price they could afford.

The hammer gun had certainly made things very much more easy for the sportsman than the muzzle-loader, but now the inventive gunmakers turned to making it even easier by relieving the shooter of having to cock the hammer. The first of the so called hammerless guns were those which used Murcott's system [figure 112], patented in 1871: the internal hammers were cocked by pressing forward the lever under the trigger guard which also drew back the bolt from the lumps and allowed the barrels to fall open. This system was simple and no extra force was needed to bring the barrels up to close the gun, as we find in the later hammerless actions. Other actions were designed, the most important of which was that patented by Anson and Deeley in 1875 and brought on the market by Westley Richards. This action, with its strength and simplicity, forms the basis for almost all modern boxlock guns; its pins extend through the action to both the locks.

110 John Buckle, head keeper at Merton, Norfolk 1887 from a photograph, Badminton Library *Shooting* 1887

111 Four of the finest shots in England *c.* 1880 Maharajah Duleep Singh standing, Lord Huntingfield left, Lord Ripon centre, Lord Walsingham right

112 Mechanism of Murcott's hammerless gun, patented in 1871. The internal hammers were cocked by the forward movement of the lever

115 Partridge driving 1880s. Note the beaters with white flags in the distance and sportsman with his loader in the foreground. Woodcut from Badminton Library *Shooting* 1887

A variety of other designs followed and the best of these are contained in the actions of today's traditional guns. In these the work of cocking the tumblers or internal hammers is done by the barrels acting as a lever either on the downward or upward movement, or both.

When hammerless guns began to take over from the hammer guns in the 1880s there were some sportsmen who naturally disliked not being able to see at a glance which barrel had been fired. As a result, some early hammerless guns have indicators on the outside of the lock; Scott's gun even had little round windows in the lock-plate so that the shooter could see the position of the tumbler. An important aspect of the hammerless gun was its safety bolt. All hammerless guns were at full cock when closed, so it was vital that the triggers were bolted. The best guns also had an intercepting block between the tumbler and the striker to prevent the gun being jarred off by a fall.

The hammerless gun had reached a highly developed stage, but there was one problem still facing the gunmakers – that of relieving the sportsman from the task of pulling the empty cartridges clear of the extractors. The first ejector mechanism for shot-guns was designed by J. Needham in 1874; Deeley's ejector, in 1884, was followed by many

114 Close up view of the breech of an Anson and Deeley boxlock ejector double-barrelled 12 bore gun made by Westley Richards c. 1885

others. By the 1890s their application had become general.

Not all shooters were won over by hammerless guns. A number of the greatest game shots, including Lord Ripon, Lord Walsingham and King George v, continued to use their hammer guns, or later had others specially built and fitted with ejectors by James Purdey in the 1890s; these had back action locks and Whitworth steel barrels [figure 115].

Other sportsmen had had second thoughts about choke bored guns. When these first appeared they thought only of the advantage of a close pattern at long ranges. However they were soon to discover that, for most normal types of shooting, too much choke led either to a miss or a bird so raked with shot that it was inedible. A popular compromise was to have a cylinder or only a slight degree of choke in the right hand barrel and a larger degree in the left. Lord Walsingham, the celebrated shot who on one occasion in 1888 shot 1,056 grouse in a day, used nothing but cylinder bored hammer guns.

In the 1880s steel barrels began to replace the beautifully figured Damascus barrels. The best were those made of Sir Joseph Whitworth's fluid pressed steel. This steel was of high quality and was so named because it was poured into the ingot and subjected to powerful pressure to eliminate flaws caused by contraction on cooling. After the introduction of steel barrels it was quickly appreciated that the lump and barrel could be forged together. These were called chopperlump barrels and the best guns were fitted with them.

In the 1880s it became the fashion to set up shooting schools on some gunmaker's shooting grounds. This development was made practicable by the use of early forms of 'clay pigeon' traps: the 'clays' were in fact made of pitch and replaced the earlier glass balls filled with feathers and some early clay targets.

A pioneer of these shooting schools was the eminent gunmaker Charles Lancaster, who in 1889 wrote an excellent and delightfully illustrated book called *The Art of Shooting* [figure 117]. One of the illustrations shows Annie Oakley receiving instruction from Charles Lancaster when she visited England in 1887 with Buffalo Bill's Wild West show [figure 116]. In a letter to Lancaster in 1888 she wrote:

Dear Sir, — The four breech-loading hammerless guns you built for me are, in my opinion, as near perfection as it is possible to get them. The pair of 20-bores (weight 5lbs.2ozs.), I have been using now nearly two years. I find them just as tight and sound as when new; I have never had any repairs except having the

115 One of Lord Ripon's hammer ejector guns built 1894, with back action locks, 30 inch Whitworth steel barrels, one of the pair

locks cleaned. The pair of 12-bores (6 lbs.) are as good as the 20s. Since using your guns, and receiving a few lessons from you at your splendid private shooting grounds, my shooting in the field has so much improved that now I always make a good score, even at fast and difficult birds. With many thanks for the pains you have taken in making me such perfect fitting and fine shooting guns.

I am, gratefully yours,
(Signed) ANNIE OAKLEY,
(Little Sure Shot).

In sporting rifles, breech-loading had solved the problem of fitting a bullet tightly into the grooves. With the muzzle-loaders, this had been done only with great difficulty and at the risk of spoiling the bullet's shape. Few pinfire rifles were made with large bores, principally because the actions were not then strong enough to stand the strain of powerful charges [figure 121]. However, with centre fire ignition, the brass-cased cartridge and the powerful screw-type under-lever grip, nothing prevented the development of a wide range of double sporting rifles from the eight-bore [figure 120] to smaller bore, high velocity, 'express' rifles. Four-bore

116 From *The Art of Shooting* by C. Lancaster, 1889. Annie Oakley practising at clay pigeons

117 From *The Art of Shooting.* Walking up through turnips – crossing to the right

rifles were made with fairly short single barrels to improve their balance and make them more manageable. However, the tendency was towards smaller bores, using elongated bullets and powerful charges: high velocity compensated for the lighter bullets. There was great interest in rifles of all types at this time, and gunmakers were equally inventive in developing the sporting rifle as they had been in perfecting the shotgun. By the 1880s and 90s they had become precision instruments which could be loaded as easily as guns: they used various actions which included the drop down opening similar to, but stronger than, those in shotguns, and the falling block and Martini mechanisms. The sportsman had a wide range of choice from the big game rifles to the very accurate deer rifles and graceful little rook and rabbit rifles. In addition, he had cartridges that had an accurately weighed powder charge.

One of the last of the great English hunters who earned a living by hunting elephants for ivory and animals for museum specimens, was Frederick Courtney Selous. He reached Southern Africa, in 1871, to find most of the old hunting grounds cleared. He headed his waggons northward in search of the last big herds of elephants in Mashonaland. In a letter to George Gibbs, who built Baker's first rifle, Selous says that the excellent .461 Gibbs-Metford

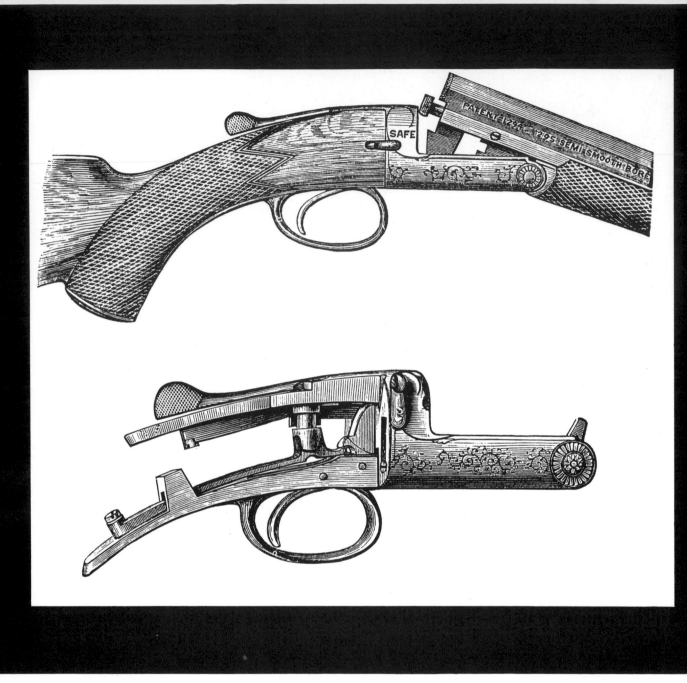

118 Holland and Holland's hammerless rook rifle, 1880s. These graceful rifles were very popular around this time

breech-loading rifle was the only one he used during his powder had disadvantages since it was some time before its ballistics were fully understood and its performance stabilized in varying conditions. Certain of the new powders gave dangerously high pressures and a number of guns burst either from the nature of the powder itself or its varying pressure under peculiar climatic and other conditions. Some sportsmen, however, did not appreciate that the old rules which had governed the bulk measures and grain sizes of

119 Diana in tweeds, from *The Art of Shooting*. C. Lancaster 1889. A few women shot at this period — some with considerable success

last twelve years in Africa. Wherever there was game, there could be found sportsmen trying to emulate the exploits of the early hunters. But these later men had vastly superior weapons, enjoyed better travelling facilities, and benefited from the experience of those who had gone before. East Africa provided some of the best of the later hunting grounds in Africa, and up to the Second World War, it was to become the home of highly organized and lavishly equipped big game safaris. These were in sharp contrast to

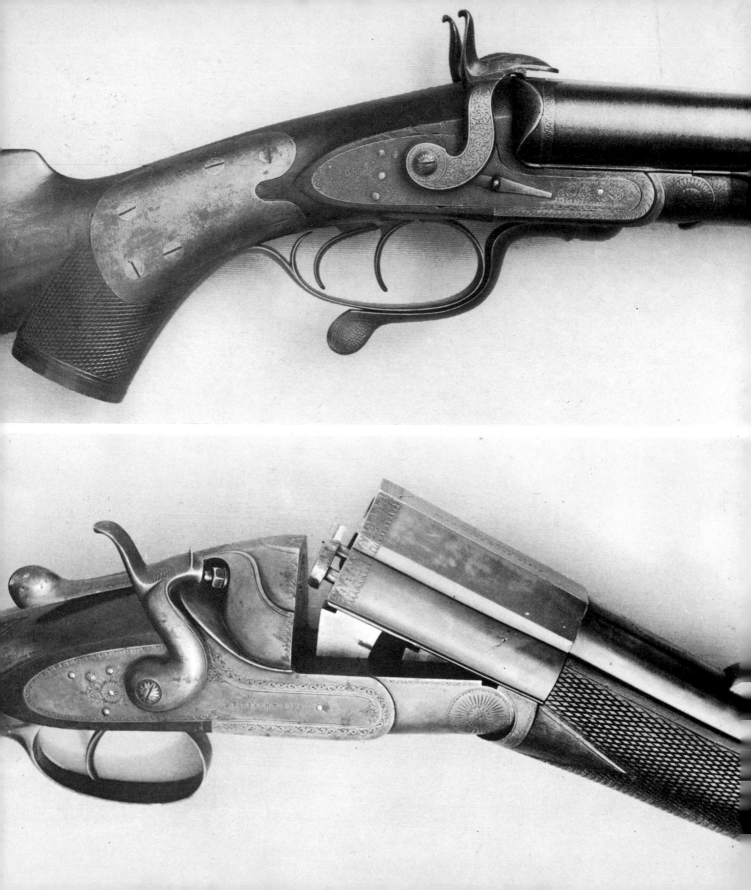

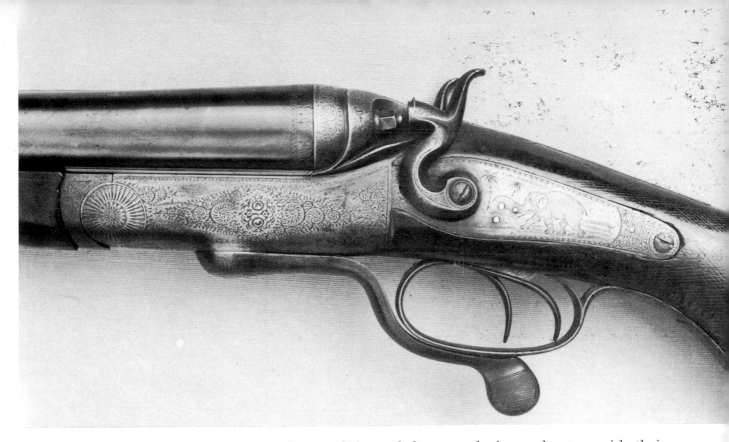

120 (*above*) Centre fire double 8 bore rifle by C. G. Bonehill, Birmingham *c.* 1880, weight 16 lbs

121 (*above left*) Pinfire double 10 bore rifle by John Rigby, Dublin and London *c.* 1860, weight 11 lbs

122 (*left*) Bland's smooth bore breech loading jungle gun. 8 bore ball and 10 drams powder

the expeditions of the rugged pioneer hunters with their muzzle-loaders.

An important development in the 1870s and 80s was the introduction of smokeless powder. This helped sportsmen a great deal, since they could now keep the target in view when they put in a second shot. Dangerous animals were no longer obscured by smoke at critical moments. This early black powder, were no longer applicable to these new powders.

One of the safest and most popular of the early nitro powders was known as Schultze after its inventor, Captain E. Schultze, who was a Prussian officer. This powder had a wood fibre base, and, because its bulk was approximately equal to that of the equivalent of black powder, no confusion in using it was liable to arise. By the end of the century nitro powders were sufficiently reliable and stable to come into general use, but for the average sportsman, cartridge loading was still best left to specialist firms who understood the precise requirements for a balanced and effective load. In 1894 that great game shot Lord Ripon was finally persuaded to stop using his favourite No 2 Black powder in favour of Schultze; up to this date he had found that the speed and the reliability of black powder amply compensated for the necessary delay in firing the second barrel.

In America much attention had been given to the development of repeating rifles which were suited to the needs of the frontier.

The Spencer repeating rifle with the magazine in the butt was patented in 1860, and was one of the earliest rifles of this kind to be successful. It was followed by the Henry, Winchester, Colt and Marlin repeating rifles operated by the well known under lever action and having the magazine under the barrel. Some models were adapted for sporting purposes and although widely used for American game, they lacked the power to deal effectively with the dangerous animals of India and Africa.

Following the success of the rifles, the system was adapted to shot guns. The Spencer action, with the cartridges in a magazine under the barrel, was operated by a sliding movement of the left hand grip. The famous pigeon shot Dr Carver demonstrated the shooting of these guns when he visited England in 1882. In 1887 the Winchester repeater was introduced with a similar action to the Winchester rifle. No doubt these repeating guns were widely used for a certain type of shooting, particularly duck flighting. In Britain, however, they were considered unsporting for game shooting, and were unpopular in company as they could not be carried open like a normal shot gun, which can be seen to be unloaded when so carried.

123 The author shown out shooting with one of the hammer-ejector guns made for Lord Ripon, the famous game shot

124 Duck shooting from a boat in a snow-storm, 1880s

125 (*opposite*) Sir Ralph Payne Gallwey, Sportsman and writer equipped for wildfowling. Woodcut from Badminton Library *Shooting*, 1887

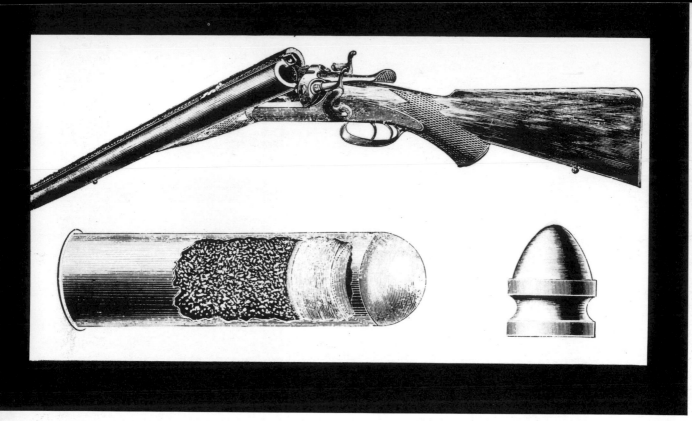

126 8 bore Elephant gun and cartridge
c. 1880. The cartridge loaded with 10 drams
of black powder

127 (*opposite top*) Late nineteenth century
trade label of Stephen Grant and Sons

128 (*opposite below*) Late nineteenth century
trade label of Messrs Boss and Co

Around the turn of the century a renewed interest was
taken in single trigger mechanisms and a number of reliable
ones were developed. They were a mixed blessing and their
popularity has risen and fallen ever since. Double guns were
made again with one barrel above, rather than to the side of
the other; this style had been used in earlier times. These
over and under guns achieved a limited popularity as game
guns, but in recent years they have been much favoured by
'clay pigeon' enthusiasts. There has also been a tendency
since the turn of the century towards lighter guns with
shorter barrels, and towards the greater use of precision tools
in gun manufacture.

It is good to know that, even in this era of mass production, hand built guns can still be ordered in London to meet
a sportsman's particular requirements. Gunmakers will care-
fully fit and stock them to suit the man's physique, and will
engrave them to order [figure 95].

Two world wars have transformed the sporting scene;
tastes and opinions have also changed. Even if the highly
organized shoots of the past were resumed, it is doubtful
whether any would welcome a return to a system where
massive bags were made by a privileged few. There are
increasing numbers of sportsmen today who are content with

129 Anson and Deeley boxlock ejector gun by Westley Richards shown in its case with spare barrels and equipment *c.* 1885

130 Under lever, hammer gun with Damascus barrels by James Woodward 1873

131 Hammerless ejector pigeon gun, with Whitworth steel barrels by James Woodward 1901

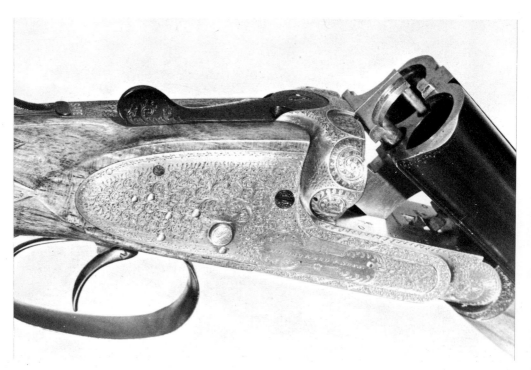

small bags and who enjoy walking up their game in fields and woods, as well as those who thrive on hopes of a chance at duck or goose on some desolate marsh.

When Lord Ripon looked back to a time before the luxurious Edwardian shooting parties, he recalled men who worked hard for their sport and who were satisfied with a sandwich for their lunch. Those were better and healthier days, he thought; the young men were keener sportsmen then. Nowadays, fortunately, the emphasis is again on keenness, and shooters have a feeling for the land and for nature which is a much a part of the true sportsman as his marksmanship. A recent development is the interest, not only in collecting old sporting guns but also in shooting with them. What better way of establishing a link between the sportsmen of the present and past!

MARKHAM, GERVASE. *Hunger's Prevention or the whole art of fowling by water and land*, London, 1621

COX, NICHOLAS. *The Gentleman's Recreation, London, 1674*. R. Blome's edition, 1686

MARKLAND, GEORGE. *Pteryflegia, or The art of shooting flying*, Dublin and London, 1727

RIDINGER, JOHANN ELIAS. *Abbildungen der Jagtbaren Thiere*, Augsburg, 1740

Der Vollkommene deutsche Jäger, Leipzig, 1724

THORNHILL, RICHARD. *The Shooting Directory*, London, 1804

GENERAL HANGER, GEORGE. *To all sportsmen, farmers and game-keepers*, London, 1814

COLONEL HAWKER, PETER. *Instructions to young Sportsmen in all that relates to Guns and Shooting*, London, 1824 and later editions

CAPTAIN LACY, *The Modern Shooter*, London, 1842

GREENER, W. *Gunnery in 1858*, London, 1858

WALSH, J. H. *The shot gun and sporting rifle, Stonehenge*, London, 1858

FOLKARD, H. C. *The Wildfowler*, 2nd edition London, 1864 and later editions

BAKER, SIR, SAMUEL WHITE. *The Rifle and Hound in Ceylon*, London, 1892

GREENER, W. W. *The Gun and its development*, London, 1881, nine editions

BADMINTON LIBRARY. *Shooting*, Vols 1 and 2 1885 and later editions

LEVESSON, H. A. C. *The hunting grounds of the old world, The Old Shekarry*, London 1868

TEASDALE-BUCKELL. *Experts on Guns and Shooting*, London, 1900

NEAL, W. KEITH. *Spanish Guns and Pistols*, G. Bell and Sons, 1956

GEORGE, J. N. *English Guns and Rifles*, The Stackpole Co. Pennsylvania, 1947 and later editions

NEAL, W. KEITH, and BACK, D. H. L. *The Mantons*, Herbert Jenkins, London, 1967

LANCASTER, CHARLES. *The Art of Shooting*, Atkin Grant and Lang Ltd, London, 1889, 13th edition, 1962

AKEHURST, RICHARD. *Game guns and rifles: percussion to hammerless ejector*, G. Bell and Sons, London, to be published 1968 or 1969